Prai

Mark was a critical hire at a critical time for Kobo. We knew independent publishing was a growing phenomenon in eBooks but needed the right person to create that all-important bridge with the author community. Mark performed that role perfectly, winning authors over to *Kobo Writing Life* with his combination of energy, lived experience as an author, genuine enthusiasm for how technology could extend a writer's reach. A truly valuable person.
— Michael Tamblyn, *CEO at Rakuten Kobo, Inc.*

Mark was a regular guest speaker for our students in the Creative Writing Program, at SFU Continuing Studies. His talks balanced providing encouraging information with the business realities of publishing. Our writers went away feeling excited about the publishing opportunities available to them, but also understood that though it is simple to publish through KWL or Amazon, success requires hard work. I personally enjoyed each one of Mark's presentations and would learn something new each time.
— Andrew Chesham, *Simon Fraser University*

His broad knowledge of publishing provided me with valuable contacts, reference materials and a couple of great ideas to move my writing and publishing projects forward. I highly recommend any way you can find time to spend with him - great value at half the price you'd expect!
— Mark Jones, *Author*

Mark is a pro. His decades of experience and continuing relevance (staying on the leading edge of publishing is no small feat in this climate) is a major asset to anyone looking to improve their position in the market...and not drive themselves insane in the process. That is gold. He is genuine, innovative, smart and seriously easy to work with. Highly recommend booking his 20-minute free consult, it can change everything.
— Sarah Kades, *Author*

Other Books in this Series

Killing It on Kobo

Leverage Insights to Optimize Publishing and Marketing Strategies, Grow Global Sales and Increase Revenue on Kobo

The 7 P's of Publishing Success

What seven traits do the most successful authors have in common? Which strategic approaches have the most impact? Where should you focus for maximum success?

AN AUTHOR'S GUIDE TO WORKING WITH LIBRARIES & BOOKSTORES

MARK LESLIE LEFEBVRE

Stark Publishing Solutions

Stark Publishing Solutions
An Imprint of Stark Publishing
Waterloo, Ontario
www.starkpublishing.ca

Publisher's Note: This work is derived from the author's experience
in bookselling, writing, and publishing, and is meant to inform and
inspire writers with tools and strategies for success in their own
writing path. The author and publisher believe that there is no single
magic solution for everyone, and that advice, wisdom and insights
should be carefully curated and adapted to suit each individual's
needs, goals and desires. In addition, the information provided was
researched in the Fall of 2019. Be aware that the platforms mentioned
are prone to change.

A list of online resources mentioned in this book can be found at:
www.markleslie.ca/authorsbookstoreslibraries

An Author's Guide to Working with Libraries & Bookstores / Mark
Leslie Lefebvre
December 2019

Print ISBN: 978-1-989351-06-2
eBook ISBN: 978-1-989351-07-9
Audio ISBN: 978-1-989351-08-6

This book is dedicated to two amazing people whose masterful passion and brilliant example inspired, informed, and enlightened me in my own bookish ways. For Doug Minette, a brilliant bookseller mentor. And in Memory of Margaret Houghton, librarian extraordinaire.

Table of Contents

INTRODUCTION: A Room of One's Own Books

AS A WRITER you have never had as many options, control, or choices than at any other time in the history of publishing.

Because in today's digital age of publishing, it's very easy to assume control and publish your book.

It's as simple as having a document in the right format and loading it directly via a retail platform or through a distributor. The tools to do that are free, and with minimal fuss, your book can be listed on all the major eBook retail platforms. In addition, you can easily get that book listed in numerous library systems.

When it comes to print books, you can use similar platforms to make your book available through the global market using POD (print on demand) services. This will make your print book available in online retail book shops as well as available for sale to libraries.

There is a similar process for audiobooks.

All of this, of course, is for online listings only – a significant, and continually growing part of the book industry. But it is still a relatively small portion of the overall industry.

It's one thing to see your book listed in an online retail or library catalog. But what about the dream of having your book on bookstore shelves? What about the feeling of being a featured author doing a book event with a stack of books on the table in front of you and a line up of readers eager to connect with you to get that book signed?

As of the writing of this book, industry statistics report that in North America upwards of 70% to 80% of people who read still read print books. The stats also indicate that the most common method for people to find out about print books isn't an online listing, it's through recommendations from friends and family.

While more purchases are happening online, one of the top ways that people still learn about new books to read is by seeing them on shelves and displays, and physically touching and holding those books in libraries and in bookstores.

This is not to mention the incredible social currency that comes with the in-person and physical connection that can happen between an author and a reader. A personal connection that, like the writing itself, can transcend the page.

Because there's something truly special when a reader has the opportunity to interact with a writer whose books they cherish.

Even if you have already achieved online and digital success, if you are pulling in a respectable income, perhaps enough to make a living as a full-time writer, if you are hitting online bestseller lists and you have readers from around the world, there are legacy systems within the book industry related to physical distribution that aren't as straightforward or seemingly easy to navigate.

Getting your book onto bookstore and library shelves or making those magical in person connections that can come from working with libraries and bookstores might seem really appealing, but so frustratingly out of reach.

But, I'm here to tell you it's not out of reach.

It's something you can have.

I have written this book to provide you with an understanding of those parts of the book industry and to help you navigate that perceived gap. And to show you that with a bit of work, a bit of learning, a bit of research, and a lot of determination, you can have those things too.

I've worked in the book industry since the early 1990s and I'm going on thirty years of experience working in virtually every type of bookstore that exists. I've worked at mall stores, big box stores, academic bookstores, independent bookstores, online bookstores, and digital eBook and audiobook bookstores.

In addition, as a board member of *BookNet Canada*, an organization that develops technology, standards, and education to serve the Canadian book industry, I have collaborated with colleagues who represented other types of bookstores and library channels. And of course, being a giant book nerd, I have always spent a lot of time in bookstores and libraries.

This book is my attempt to share the things I have experienced and learned about bookstores and libraries with you, to help empower you with information that you can use in order to succeed in that print-focused realm of the book industry.

If you have been an author for a while you will likely already be familiar with some of the basic elements I describe and walk through in the early sections of each chapter. Those may be elements you choose to skip over; or perhaps you might use them as a refresher to your own experience. But it was important for me to include them in order to make this book as complete, informative, and useful whether you are an experienced author, or you are just beginning.

In a similar way, I provide insights and strategies for both traditionally published and self-published authors, so that you can find value and understand your options regardless of how you have approached your path into the book world.

But regardless of the logistics of where you are on your own author journey or how your books are published, this book should present you with insights, ideas, and inspiration that you can use to grow and enhance your own interactions with bookstores and libraries.

So, if you're ready, take my virtual hand, and follow me on to the next page, where we can begin to explore all of these options and opportunities together.

MODUS OPERANDI: The Basics of How Libraries & Bookstores Work

THERE IS A QUOTE that has been in the footer of my personal email for well over a decade. It's from Marcus Tullius Cicero, a Roman philosopher, and it reads: "A room without books is like a body without a soul."

I cherish the quote because it reflects my life-long love affair with books, with writing, and, for my entire post-secondary education life, working in the book industry.

But one thing that writers can often forget, when thinking about the romantic notion of a room filled with books, is that bookstores and libraries are businesses, each fulfilling a specific need within their communities.

Bookstores are retail businesses. Yes, there are different models, which we will get to later in this book. But, at their core, once you strip off the passion for books that is often what drew us as authors and them as booksellers, into that realm, they are a retail operation. They rent a space in order to bring in products, try to sell those products to a specific clientele, and, if that product doesn't sell, they'll want a way to dispose of the product, either by returning it or having to write that product down and liquidate those assets.

It seems cold when you think about the fact that we are talking about books. But it is important to remember. If a bookstore doesn't earn more money selling books than it spends on rent, supplies, and labor costs, it can't remain in operation.

Libraries serve their community by offering information, services, and reading material to their patrons. Their funding often comes from local, state, or provincial taxes, usually via some sort of cultural funding operation that is centrally controlled.

A library's success, when it comes to books, is measured by the turn-over and use of its stock by patrons. For books, a library cares not about sales, but about books their patrons will read. Books that are read are important assets to continue to stock, or to replenish when the stock wears out. Books that aren't read are eventually removed from stock.

When it comes to reading and to books, though they are different types of operations, the basic concern is often the same. Every day they look for an answer to this fundamental question: *How can we put the right book into the right reader's hands at the right time?*

There are many other details and operational procedures that go well beyond that which we will explore together in the following pages. Such as details and specifics of how it happens, the source of information, the processes that exist, and the people who fulfill different roles.

But before we do that, I want you to always keep this critical and fundamental underlying goal in mind, because that's what we as authors ultimately want to assist them with: *The right book in the right reader's hands at the right time.*

WORKING WITH BOOKSTORES

IN 1992, THE same year that I graduated from Carleton University in Ottawa with my Honors Degree in English Language and Literature, and also saw my very first short story in print, I took my first part-time job as a bookseller. My life-long passion for books and for writing seemed to be gestating nicely.

A part-time seasonal position in a bookstore for the Christmas season was the first of many stepping stones that I made throughout the book industry.

Between 1992 and 1999 I worked in five different bookstore locations in Ottawa and Hamilton Ontario, learning all about the front line of the retail book trade; from customer interactions, to managing inventory stock and personnel, working with publishing sales representatives, and the logistics of receiving, stocking, and returning books.

In 1999 I moved to work for Chapters Online, Canada's first major online bookstore. There I learned about the importance of accurate and efficient metadata, the information that feeds to and from publishers, as well as the logistical operation for managing the data and processes for Canada's largest book warehouse, and the challenges of a 24/7 online bookstore operation.

That role led to working at the head office of Chapters, which was bought by and absorbed into Indigo Books and Music, Inc. There, I continued to work at processing, importing and strategically sharing the critical information needed about books to feed both an always open online bookstore, but also the needs of the head office book buyers and the operation of putting stock into hundreds of big box and smaller mall stores across the country. Among the wonderful learnings there, I spearheaded the creation of an online tool that would allow smaller publishers the ability to work with Canada's largest bookseller despite these publishers not having an IT department or the technical ability to provide the data in the fully automated data industry standard terms.

In 2006, I moved back to the front line of bookselling, this time managing the book operations for an academic bookstore at McMaster University. In many ways, this part of the book industry was completely new and different than the one I had grown up on, so I relished learning about an entirely new side of the book industry, including the fundamental differences of the way that textbooks and academic reading material is sourced, bought and sold. In addition to the usual shipping and receiving, inventory management, and metadata fields, there were entirely unique data fields needed for additional purposes of faculty members needing to share required and optional reading lists to classrooms. I also learned about the used book business, and got my first taste at running a printing operation by leveraging an in-store print on demand business using an Espresso Book Machine.

In 2011, I was hired by Kobo, Canada's scrappy little digital book upstart, and tasked with coming up with a solution that would allow Kobo to work with self-published authors. It was a parallel to the online system I had built many years earlier for small publishers wanting to work with Chapters/Indigo; but this time it wasn't for the information required to order, stock and sell physical books online in Canada, or for shipping to one of the chain's stores, it was for the ingestion of both metadata and the actual eBooks themselves for retail sale to a global market.

In 2018, I applied all the things I had learned about empowering independently published authors at Kobo and began a part-time contract position with *Draft2Digital*, an Oklahoma based company that distributes eBooks to all the major retail and library systems.

All this is to say that, my experience, since 1992, has allowed me a plethora of insights into the logistical, operational, and functional operations of almost every type of bookstore.

Compressing all that info gathered over decades into a relatively short book is a challenge that I don't take lightly.

But I have done my best to filter it down to the things that I think are important for an author to understand for working with various types of bookstore environments.

In addition, I have made every effort to divide this chapter into segments to perhaps match the type of specific information you might require. This should allow you to skip things you don't need to worry about – such as, if you have a handle on the basics of listing your books – and move on to another area that is useful to you at the particular stage you are at in your own unique author journey as it relates to bookstores.

Ideally, if it all works as intended, when you finish with this chapter, you will be fully equipped and confident in your own ability to interact and engage with bookstores efficiently, effectively and in a professional manner.

The Basics

The first few sections that follow are going to focus on the very basics of listing your books. They aren't going to get into any specific "how-to" details.

This book is **not** going to explain:

- How to find an agent or publishing within traditional publishing
- How to do any of the specific steps of setting up your book

- How to find a good editor or a book cover designer for your book
- How to get an ISBN (or the debate of owning your own VS using ones assigned by a distributor/retailer)
- Any of the costs or mechanics associated with either of the previous two points above

There are plenty of books and free online resources out there that can do many of these things for you, and there will also be links to resources in the back of this book to some of them.

However, if you are at the early phase of wanting to understand the basics of how it works for an author to get their eBook or their print book listed with bookstores, this section should be a useful primer for you.

Listing Your Books

As mentioned, this is going to be a high-level overview of how you can get your books listed in bookstore catalogs.

First, if you are a traditionally published author, then that publisher likely has warehousing, and has either direct retail sales channels relationships or is partnered with a distribution warehouse and/or sales force that will ensure your book is listed as available to bookstores. They likely are set up to sell their books through Ingram or Baker and Taylor, which are two of the largest English language wholesalers of print books that bookstores can order from.

This might suggest that you needn't worry about the listing segment, because it is likely already taken care of for you. But it might be good for you to understand a bit about the listing process, because it might be, depending on the size of the publisher you are working with, the same process to what they are doing for you.

If you are traditionally published with a publishing house that uses POD or print on demand printing, then those books might still be available to bookstores and automatically listed on the websites of the major eBook retailers, likely via Ingram's print on demand services for larger and smaller publishers. It is important to at least understand this aspect of the publisher you are working with. And I would strongly advise if you have signed the rights to a book to any publisher that you double check your contract and ask your publisher where and how bookstores can purchase their books.

Because typically, with print on demand titles, the books are set up as non-returnable from bookstores, which means that while the bookstore might list the title to be available for order via their website, or be willing to fulfill a special order for that book, they might not stock them.

Don't despair, though. I will, later on in this chapter, talk about strategies that you can use if your print book (whether self-published or traditionally published) is available POD and is non-returnable with a bookstore.

If you are self-published, then I will make the assumption that you have, at the very least, an edited and proof-read manuscript, and a book cover and book description that have been created with your ideal target reading audience in mind.

I am also going to stick with the major players in the English language market, and not delve beyond what some might construe as a very North-American, or at least primarily English language territory (US, CA, UK, AU, NZ) market approach.

Let's start with the easiest one first, eBooks.

eBooks

If you have a manuscript ready to go, it is free and easy to get your eBook listed and available for sale. Perhaps one of the more overwhelming elements of being at this phase in your author journey is the incredible amount of choice that you have.

This might sound like an odd thing to say but having too many options can actually be something that limits you – it's often referred to as "analysis paralysis."

So, in the spirit of those parents who are helping their young children with making their own first steps of choosing their own clothes when getting ready in the morning, I'm going to limit the discussion of your choice between just one or two alternatives, rather than throwing open the closet and expecting you to sift through too many options.

But you should also be aware that there is a veritable smorgasbord of options available to you.

Basically, you can choose between publishing direct to an online eBook retailer or using a third party that distributes to them.

All of the major English language eBook retailers have their own direct publishing option.

Direct Publishing Options

- Amazon - *Kindle Direct Publishing* (KDP)
- Apple Books - *Pages*
- Kobo - *Kobo Writing Life* (KWL)
- Barnes & Noble – *B&N Press*
- Google – *Google Play Partner Center*

Each of these five major online retail direct publishing platforms are free to use. They usually also have built-in the ability to convert your document into an eBook or to allow you to upload the book in eBook (ePub) format. The conversion is most often from Microsoft Word into ePub.

The way that these platforms work is that you sign an agreement with each of them that basically agrees to the following:

- You are either the original creator of this work, or you are authorized by the creator with the rights to publish this work
- You are authorizing the retailer to sell your book and you will or the publisher name/imprint you operate under, will be identified as the publisher

of this book (*NOTE: The retailer is **not** your publisher. They are merely selling your book*)

- You maintain the rights to this work and can delist or unpublish the book at any time. However, the retailer reserves the right to store, in a cloud-based system, that book for any customers who have already purchased the book or downloaded it to their personal library even after you remove it (*Think of this as being similar to the equivalent of a person who buys and still owns a print book even after a book is no longer in print*)
- Your eBook will not be set at a lower retail price on any other retailer, and that this retailer reserves the right to automatically price match should a lower price appear on any of the competitor websites
- The retailer can, at their own discretion, choose to not accept or make your eBook available for sale. They can also limit the eBook's availability in particular territories based on local laws or territorial cultural norms. Similarly, they can decide to remove your eBook from sale, for whatever reason they choose, at any time.

The way that compensation from these major retailers works is they will handle the retail sales taxes for sale of the books to the end consumer, charging the consumers the appropriate tax in their country, province, state, and remit those taxes to the applicable government agency.

You will be paid, at the end of a particular fiscal period (often a specific and pre-determined number of days after the end of a monthly, quarterly, or annual fiscal period) for the calculated revenue that you have earned from the retail sales of your eBook.

Compensation is based on a percentage of the retail price. In the majority of cases, if your book is priced between $2.99 and $9.99 USD you will receive 70%. For example, if your book sells for $9.99 USD in the United States, you will receive about $7.00 USD and the retailer will keep $3.00 USD.

If your book is priced between $0.99 and $2.99 USD, in most cases, you will receive 35% of the retail price. If, for example, you price a book at $1.00 USD, you will receive $0.35 USD.

And, specifically on Amazon, if your book is priced above $9.99, you will earn 35% instead of 70%. For example, if you price a book at $20.00 USD on Amazon, you will receive $7.00. Notice how, on Amazon in particular, this is pretty much the same amount of money you would earn on a book at half of that price.

There are, in addition, slight variances in the different retailers. For example, *Kindle Direct Publishing* will also include a surcharge to any book priced within the $2.99 to $9.99 USD category based on the file size of your eBook. (The "bigger" your file, the higher the surcharge). This fee is usually tiny, a matter of pennies, and would result in you actually receiving an odd percentage, such as 69.73% rather than 70%.

In addition, for *Kobo Writing Life*, your books priced between $0.99 and $2.99 USD will earn 45% instead of 35%.

And, via *Kobo Writing Life*, Apple Books *Pages*, and *B&N Press*, there is no price cap for 70%. A $20.00 USD book published direct via those retailers would earn you $14.00 USD.

** Please note that in VAT-inclusive countries, where the tax is included in the retail price, rather than added on after the sale, the retailer will pay you the agreed upon percent **after** they back out the tax from that price.*

If you explore the details from the various direct service providers, you'll notice that some of them have options and opportunities that might only be offered to those with direct accounts with them.

You can, only, for example, run Amazon Advertising Ads on titles published to Amazon direct via *Kindle Direct Publishing*. *Kobo Writing Life* has a built-in promotions tab only for titles published direct to Kobo via that platform. (In the interest of full transparency, I created and managed *Kobo Writing Life* for the first five years of the platform's existence – I actually share as many of my insights about Kobo as possible in the book **Killing It On Kobo**). *B&N Press* offers similar perks to direct customers. Apple Books seems more open to promoting direct publishing authors as well as authors coming in from third party distributors.

And *Google Play* hasn't made many moves, other than to inconsistently throw up roadblocks to authors wanting to publish direct to their platform. But signs are out there that, just on the horizon as this book is preparing to go to press, Google will be making a play toward being more receptive to Indie authors.

Distribution Options

Instead of publishing direct to retailers, you also have the option of using a third-party distribution platform to get to those retailers.

While there are many different variances in models, I have chosen to outline them into the three main types of distribution platforms that exist.

I was tempted to break the services down into two, which I would call *Free to Publish* and *Pay to Publish*. However, there are enough variations of the pay to publish models that I further broke those down, mostly to highlight the transparency and integrity of some of the players involved.

1. **Free to Publish.**
    In this model, you can publish for free, and the distributor keeps a % of your retail price. It is similar to the model that the direct-to-retailer platforms offer, and results in the distributor keeping a small slice of the % overall margin received from the retailer.
    These companies earn money only when you successfully sell a book. Their goal is to remove the barriers to publishing for you and enable you to publish for free with minimal hassle, using a single account

instead of having to manage multiple publishing accounts at all the retailers. And, should you achieve sales and earn money, they keep a share of that money. If you earn a lot of money, their earnings grow.

2. **Pay to Publish.**
In this model, you either pay an initial fee up-front, or you pay a monthly subscription service to the platform. These platforms do not receive any cut from the % that is sent from the retailer. They pass that full margin right on to you.
These companies earn money up front regardless of whether or not you make a single sale. Their goal is to remove the barriers for publishing to make it easy for you to publish your book to multiple retail platforms using a single account, instead of having to manage multiple publishing accounts at all retailers. They earn their money up front, regardless of whether or not you make a single sale.

3. **Full-service.**
In this model, you pay for distribution, eBook conversion, and distribution. The publishing platform might also keep a percentage of your sales.
These companies earn money up front and sometimes on an ongoing basis regardless of whether or not you make a single sale. Their systems can remove the barriers for publishing, as well as assist you with some of the necessary elements (editing, design), but each of

those elements likely includes an additional cost. Their goal is to make money from your desire to publish, and, in many cases, make money from your desire to market your book in the hopes of making sales.

While there are legitimate and honest businesses who use this particular model and operate with integrity, I cannot emphasise enough that this is typically the area where most of the crooks, sharks, and sleazy players operate, and you would be well-advised to investigate the reputation of any platform using this model on sites such as "Writer Beware."

In addition, many of the businesses within this realm masquerade as "real publishers" or "traditional publishers" and often explain, on their website, the ways that they are a real publisher.

Please note that no actual and legitimate traditional publisher charges authors for editing, design, distribution, or marketing. And, in the same way that no reputable and respected leader in history has ever had to refer to themselves as a "stable genius" no legitimate publisher has ever had to call themselves a "real publisher."

In order to help illustrate the differences (which can often, on the surface appear similar), I will present below a limited number of examples of some of the companies that use the models listed above.

Free to Publish:

- *Draft2Digital*
- *Smashwords**
- *StreetLib*

There are other companies, but these are among the most well-known. With all three companies listed, you can upload your epub or Microsoft Word document and use their free eBook conversion tool and distribute to retail environments without charge. They usually keep about 10% of the revenue from the downstream retailer, meaning that, instead of you earning 70% you would earn 60%.

Draft2Digital is a US based company, and, in my opinion, the most author-centric platform with the most forgiving free Microsoft Word to eBook (ePub and mobi) formatting as well as numerous automated tools designed to save an author time and hassle. (*In the interest of full disclosure, I should acknowledge my experience working professionally with Draft2Digital to note that it's likely I have a positive bias toward this platform*)

StreetLib is a company originally from Italy that has a hearty presence in many European countries that Draft2Digital doesn't currently reach.

* *Smashwords* is a distributor but they also have their own direct retail catalog. They have a global presence that, like Kobo, reaches into countries that Amazon has no presence in. I choose not to list them as a retailer in the Direct Publishing Options listing, because they are more known for being a distribution platform rather than a retailer. But they do have a retail presence. However, it is critically important to understand how their publishing model works. They automatically select ALL downstream channels to publish to, which can be confusing for a beginning writer. Please note that once you hit the "publish" button on *Smashwords*, you need to immediately go back in and opt-out of all the retail and library channels on that eBook that you might already be published to so that you don't get duplicate listings.

Pay to Publish:
- *BookBaby*
- *PublishDrive*

Again, there are other companies operating within this model, but I thought it would be important to highlight these two because of the different ways they operate.

BookBaby, which has been around for many years, offers paid publishing services related to editing, design, formatting/eBook conversion, marketing, and distribution. They are an all-inclusive service provider with various packages available. When it comes to distribution, the author gets their full 70% earnings. *BookBaby* makes their money up front per title, and that's it.

PublishDrive, which launched a bit more recently as a *Free to Publish* platform, adjusted their model in 2019 to a more *Pay to Publish* approach; they have a complicated model that seems to continue to evolve and morph. But at the time of this writing, they offer eBook conversion and distribution using a monthly subscription model. They don't offer editing and design services. Authors pay a flat monthly fee to publish through their platform, and authors retain the full 70% earnings on their eBook sales. This model is likely not for a beginning author, but rather for an author who is earning more than $1000 USD per month on their eBook sales. (It's basic math. If a *Free to Publish* operation keeps 10% and you are earning $1000 per month, this means the *cost* of that service works out to about $100, which is one of the basic plans that *PublishDrive* offers.)

Full-Service:

- *Authoright*
- *Lulu*
- *Matador*

I only listed a few of the companies in this realm, but there are literally hundreds of them in existence. The terms and offerings of these companies all vary wildly and broadly.

The way they operate is offering editorial and design packages, distribution options, sometimes tied to specific packages, and up-sell opportunities for marketing.

This is the area where you need to proceed with extreme caution. While there are companies within this realm that operate with integrity and provide valuable resources that allow an author to focus on the writing and let other professionals take care of the things they are best at, this is also where the predators and the sharks prey on unsuspecting authors.

And, unfortunately, the lines between legitimate publishing operations and the crooks of the world have become further blurred in the past decade.

While working on the first draft of this book, I shared an excerpt from earlier in the chapter on how a legitimate publisher would never charge an author for services, and one author posted an example of just that, suggesting I had never heard of *Archway* which is operated by Simon & Schuster, one of the world's largest publishers.

Archway is a joint venture between Simon & Schuster and *Author Solutions*. *Author Solutions* is one of the largest, if not *the* largest full-service / self-publishing/vanity publishing company in the world. They own, manage, or are affiliated with these companies (among many others):

- Archway
- AuthorHive
- AuthorHouse
- BookTango
- iUniverse
- Trafford
- Xlibris

You should be wary of any company/imprint or otherwise that are in any way affiliated with *Author Solutions*. Yes, the people who work there and often the ones they contract out for editorial and design services are professionals, often experts with years of experience in the industry. But the company's overall business model is more in line with the goal of selling and up-selling services to writers, rather than actually earning money when an author is successful.

They are motivated to sell authors more services, and not to help authors be successful via retail sales.

I would strongly advise that, before working with any full-service company, to check free online resources such as *Writer Beware* and the Alliance of Independent Authors online listing of self-publishing platforms and service providers. The URLs for these sources are listed in the resource section at the end of this book.

Going Direct VS Using a Distributor

Now that we have looked at a high level overview of the different ways that you can get your books listed on the online retailers, you need to explore your own personal needs and decide what is best for you and your writing and publishing goals.

Do you prefer full control, to have access to some tools that might only be available to those who publish direct, and earn the highest revenue possible? Then perhaps having a direct account is the best thing for you. Just be aware that, on the flip side, if you end up wanting to make a change on a single book (a metadata or a price change) you'll have to log in to at least four different platforms and make the same change four times.

Or, do you understand the cost and lost margin, but prefer to have a single login/single account to log into and can make one change that will flow downstream to all the retailers? Perhaps, in that case, for you, the time spent managing multiple accounts might be worth the lost margin.

If you decide to go with a third party distributor, do you prefer the *Free to Publish* option where you can start with little risk and no need to invest cash up front, knowing that the cost will be taken out of the revenue you earn. Or do you prefer the *Pay to Publish* model where you know exactly what you're paying either up front or via a monthly or annual subscription model.

Do you need distribution and services because you don't know where to turn? How does that affect you in terms of saving time having to hunt down professionals to work with at making your book the best it can be?

There's no simple or easy answer.

There's no one answer for everyone.

The best you can do is understand the pros and cons of each system and make an informed decision.

And it's okay to decide one thing today, and to change your mind about it tomorrow because your perspective or your needs change. And it is, similarly, okay to try different models for different books.

I have, over the years, tried numerous different approaches of publishing direct versus publishing through a third-party platform, and some of my books are published via one method, while others have their own unique setup. It's not all that different than the fact that I have chosen to license the rights to some of my books via traditional publishers while keeping the rights to others to myself for self-publishing.

The right answer can and will change, not just for you, but for each of your books.

And that's okay.

The method that works best for you for any particular project today might change tomorrow as the market shifts, as retailers and distribution options evolve and change, as your goals and perspective change.

While I can't tell you what works better, as that is a question unique to each author/book combination, what I can assure you is that what's best for you is likely to change and evolve over time.

Digital Audiobooks

If you are traditionally published, and if you licenced the audio rights to your publisher, then your publisher has likely already taken care of distribution of your book in digital audio format to the major retailer and library channels.

If the publisher did attain audio rights but hasn't actually exploited them and enough time after publication date has occurred, double check to see if there is a clause about that in the contract. The clause might state that rights revert back to the author under specific conditions or timelines. However, even without such a clause, I have successfully negotiated the return of my audio rights to me back from a publisher when, after four years, there was still no audiobook produced. It was simply a matter of the fact that the publisher didn't have the means to produce the audiobook, and, if I was able to, it would create an additional entry point into that book in its different formats, potentially benefiting sales of the print and eBook editions, which the publisher had properly exploited.

If you want to self-publish your audiobook, the two main routes are with either the DIY option, or a paid audiobook creation and distribution service.

The DIY option includes having the production-ready audio files prepared to load but might also include a platform that allows you to find a professional narrator to work with.

Here are three of the most well-known DIY distribution platforms.

- *ACX (Audiobook Creation Exchange)*
- *Authors Republic*
- *Findaway Voices*

ACX is an Amazon-owned platform that allows for direct upload of the finished product as well as options for finding a narrator to work with using a self-direct RFP-style process. You can determine if you want to pay the narrator up front or to set up a royalty-sharing process. *ACX* will get your audiobook listed with Audible, Amazon, and Apple Books.

It is important to be aware that there is an option within ACX to either be exclusive (with a 7-year commitment), or non-exclusive. There are pros and cons of being locked into a single or limited number of retailers in a continually growing and expanding market.

Authors Republic is a Canadian company which was founded in 2015 and was the first way that I was aware an author could load their fully produced and completed audiobook well beyond Amazon and Apple. At the time of this writing, they distribute to 33 different retailer and library channels. They offer distribution, and though they don't offer support with having an audiobook created, they do provide a list of resources on their website.

Findaway Voices, launched in 2016, is run by Findaway, a US company that has been revolutionizing the audiobook industry since it launched in 2006. You can upload your completed audiobook for distribution, or you can use their platform to collaborate with a narrator, with choices of full payment to the narrator or royalty-splitting options. In addition, they have a few built-in promotional opportunities that include the creation of coupon codes, a partnership with BookBub's *Chirp*, and distribution strategies, such as Voices Plus, that allow for additional promotional options. At the time of this writing, they distribute to 41 different retail and library channels.

There are also a number of service-oriented audiobook platforms that will, for a fee, help you produce an audiobook and distribute it to the downstream retailer and library channels.

I am not going to list the platforms that offer this, but I do, in the resources section, provide a few online sources where you can find some.

Just be careful, in the same way I suggest for any publishing and distribution service provider, of the over-priced packages and up-sold services that some of the companies might charge. You should always approach such services with a "writer be leery" attitude, and double check their reputation through online listings from the Alliance of Independent Authors or Writer Beware.

Of the providers in this realm, I have had personal experience working with *ListenUp Audiobooks*, a US company, for both production and distribution. I connected with them via a discounted service offering in a partnership they had with *Kobo Writing Life* (which saved me $100 per finished hour on the production of the very first audiobook I produced). I have also had the pleasure of touring their Atlanta headquarter studios. I can say that my experience working with them has been smooth and consistently professional.

Print Books

There are two main ways to get your print books listed with bookstores. One is selling or licensing your rights to a publisher, and the other is self-publishing your book.

We will explore both options within this section but get into more detail within the self-publishing or DIY method, because of the intricacies and choices involved.

So, let's start with a book that you have sold to a publisher. To be completely frank about this, when the book is sold to the right publisher, that's the easiest way to ensure you have the book listed, and either already ordered and stocked, or easily available for the bookstore to order with industry standard terms that bookstores prefer.

If you have sold your rights to a publisher, be sure to check the details of the contract and also ask (if it's not already known), if the publish is a true "traditional" or "legacy" publisher, or a more digital-first publisher.

Traditional/Legacy publishers are publishers that do Offset printing and either have their own warehouse, or collaborate with warehouse distribution platforms for making their books available to the retail market.

Digital-first publishers are those publishing companies or imprints that have leveraged digital printing and eBook publishing to make their mark, and don't involve themselves with large print runs or the more physical supply chain logistics.

The two main high level options we are looking at is related to the difference between two main types of printing. For anyone well-versed in printing methods and logistics, you'll know I'm simplifying this significantly – I am doing that for the purpose of outlining the differences at a really high level.

If your publisher is using Offset printing and warehousing (either their own warehouse or using a wholesaler warehouse and distribution company); this means that your book is likely available easily and efficiently for being stocked at bookstores. Bookstores can look up and order the books via multiple different platforms. The books are likely also listed in attractive glossy print catalogs (often published quarterly in four buying season cycles). The books are sold at bookstore-friendly trade discount terms (often 40% to 55%) and are fully returnable.

When you are communicating with a bookstore, it will be important to let them know the title, format, and retail price for your book, as well as the name of the publisher, and the name of the distributor they can order the book from. In the case of formats, if there happens to be more than one format (hardcover, paperback, mass market, or even physical audio such as CD), you should be sure to include all of them. The reason I suggest this is that a book in multiple formats offers a very subtle and perhaps subconscious indication that both you and your publisher are truly serious and professional in your approach, particularly because of the investment in multiple formats. It's one of those subtle things that might make you stand out in the crowd.

If your publisher is primarily using Print on Demand (POD) for your book, then it might not have attractive discount terms (lower than 40%) and is very likely not to be returnable.

In this second case, your publisher might allow you to purchase copies of your book directly for a discount of 40% or greater, which means that you might be able to use that for providing local bookstores with access to your titles using direct consignment models. This would be almost no different than the type of negotiations you might make with a bookstore for a title that you are doing yourself and using POD options for.

Examples of Digital VS Offset Printers

Stark Publishing. This is the imprint that I created in 2004 when I self-published my very first book, *One Hand Screaming.* I used *Ingram Lightning Source* to make the POD version available, and initially set it up as fully returnable with the highest discount possible. I have published more than a dozen print books using this imprint, which is mostly used for my own titles. This is an example of self-publishing using POD for distribution.

WordFire Press. This US publisher, owned and operated by Kevin J. Anderson and Rebecca Moesta, is used for many of their own titles, but they also acquire rights from authors, with no advance, but very author-friendly terms and clauses, and higher royalties than you'll likely ever see from larger legacy publishers. WordFire Press primarily uses POD distribution for their titles. However, they did publish a single title with mass appeal in 2019 that needed Offset printing and warehousing, but 99% of their operation is an example of an indie publisher using POD for distribution.

Dundurn Press. This Canadian publisher is the largest independent publisher in Canada (Independent means that it isn't owned by any of the "Big Five" publishers). Their contracts are legacy publisher contracts, with an advance and minimal royalties. And their distribution is primarily using warehouse and storing, with UTP (University of Toronto Press) Distribution for warehousing and shipping their books to outlets across Canada. They also occasionally also use POD for some of their distribution beyond Canada.

If I were to set up a book signing at a bookstore, the approach to that would be significantly different depending on which of these three publishers my book was made available with. In the case of Dundurn, the ordering and returns and all those logistics are taken care of. For the case of WordFire and Stark Publishing, it's a little trickier; but – and this is important to understand – not impossible with the right attitude and approach. I'll talk more about that later in this chapter.

Direct Publishing Options

- (Amazon) - *KDP Print*
- (Barnes & Noble) - *Barnes and Noble Press*

In English language markets, particularly with a North American centric focus, there aren't many options for publishing to a retail platform direct. I have listed two here.

It's important to note that, while both are US companies, one of them (Amazon) has a huge global presence, and is available in all the major English language markets that include the US, Canada, the UK, Australia, and New Zealand, while the other (Barnes and Noble) is a US-only market.

Both of these platforms offer POD printing, and they each have their own unique benefits.

The benefit of publishing direct to a retail market is that you will typically earn more because of the fact that you are eliminating the "middle-man." Essentially, the less people who are taking a cut of the pie, the more money there is for the publisher. (In this case, you are the publisher).

The downside of publishing direct to a retail market is the fact that it makes your book available **only** to that one retailer. And that is why it is important for authors to consider using a distribution option that supplies to multiple bookstores.

KDP Print, or *Kindle Direct Publishing Print*, is built into the same account you would use when publishing your eBook direct to Amazon. When you log in and go to your bookshelf you will see the option to start with either a paperback or an eBook. If you have an existing eBook, the option to create a paperback will exist.

Given that Amazon is the world's largest bookstore, and one of the largest search engines used on the internet, many authors who are self-publishing will already have their eBook available on Amazon through *KDP*. Setting up the print version of their book is that much easier, since much of the same metadata can be used, saving a bit of manual entry time.

The service is free to use, and they only make money from the print book when someone buys your book. So, one would assume that they have a vested interest in selling your book. And, while it has never been officially stated as a company policy, it does make sense that, since Amazon would earn more from a book published direct from their internal service than they would earn on a POD book submitted to them from a third party, they are very likely to favor books published direct.

Marketing opportunities on Amazon via Amazon Advertising (formerly AMS – Amazon Marketing Services) can only be used on Amazon.com, Amazon.co.uk, or Amazon.de for titles that are published directly to Amazon via *KDP*.

For *Barnes and Noble Press*, in the most basic of cases, and, as stated on their website, your friends and fans can order your print book from any B&N store across the country—all they have to do is ask, and the store will then place an order and the book will ship directly to the customer. It doesn't even go through the stores.

B&N also comes with unique merchandising opportunities. For example, if you sell more than 1,000 copies of your eBook in a 12-month period, you become eligible to pitch the print version of that book (also published via *Barnes and Noble Press*) to B&N store buyers. If the book is selected by them, it will be stocked in Barnes and Noble bookstores across the country.

Similarly, authors who sell more than 500 copies of a *Barnes & Noble Press* eBook in a 12-month period are eligible to host an in-store event.

Barnes and Noble Press also lists various exclusive marketing programs designed to offer authors with awareness and sales via online promotions, monthly themed curated collections, special featured deals and promotions on BN.com, and Email newsletter marketing to B&N customers featuring genres and deals.

You'll notice that there is very specific favoritism placed by the retailers on authors using their publish-direct platform, for both print and eBook options.

Additional Notes about KDP Print & Createspace

It is important to be aware that, while I have listed *KDP Print* as a direct publishing option, it does come with an *extended distribution* option.

While I believe that *KDP Print* is an excellent solution for direct publishing your print book to Amazon, I also know that it isn't the best solution for getting your print books into the broader book market.

This is because *KDP Print* offers unattractive and very uncompetitive terms to bookstores; your books are automatically made non-returnable and are given a short discount, and, you, as the publisher, have no ability to modify these terms that mark your book, in the eyes of most booksellers, as less desirable.

Even though bookstores pride themselves on special orders for their customers, I know that the idea of ordering a book from Amazon, the massive giant that has displaced many independent bookstores, puts them off.

Consider this from the bookstore's perspective. It would be like saying: "Hello local neighborhood bookstore. Please support me by ordering my book from (and giving your money to) the same giant company that has displaced you and tried to put you out of business for the past few decades." How would you feel in their shoes?

I often refer to Amazon KDP Print's *extended distribution* option as "pretended distribution" – because it gives authors the impression that they are actually reaching a global print market. And, while their books might be listed as available, they are also listed with terms that are good only for Amazon.

In addition, you might hear people refer to *Createspace* when talking about using POD direct to Amazon, particularly if their POD experience happened prior to 2019. *Createspace* was originally founded in 2000 in South Carolina under the name *BookSurge*. They were acquired by Amazon in 2005. Beginning in 2018, that operation was slowly migrated and transferred from a separate login and access and merged into the master *KDP* dashboard. Based on my own experiences comparing

Createspace and *KDP Print* (as well as speaking with hundreds of authors who have used both), I can say that *Createspace* was far superior in terms of title management and customer service. That's about all I'm going to bother mentioning, but I did want to include mention of what happened to *Createspace*, since it's very likely that you will hear it come up when interacting in certain author circles.

Distribution Options

There are hundreds of POD distribution options that will get your book listed with bookstores. Many of them fall under the same "writer beware" category that I mentioned in the earlier section in this chapter about eBook distribution. So, I am not going to repeat that here, but I do want to be one hundred percent clear that these are shark-infested waters. Before you agree to sign up with anyone for POD services, double-check the terms you are giving up, and do a little online research to see what websites like the Alliance of Independent Authors (Alli) and the website "Writer Beware!" from Victoria Strauss. (You will find the URLs for these sites listed in the resource section at the end of this book).

Instead, I'm just going to list and talk about a handful of them, in two groups.

The first group are a couple of full-service POD distribution platforms. I personally don't use these, because I would rather manage the hiring of editors, designers, formatting, etc, on my own. But I recognize that not all authors have the patience or fortitude to find the professionals that can help them.

- *Lulu*
- *BookBaby*

I have known authors who have used *Lulu* and been pleased, particularly about the quality of their print offering. And they offer a range of DIY options as well as packages that start at $99 and go up to thousands of dollars. Authors will have to pay any time they want to make updates to their print books.

The main thing that makes me leery about a service like *Lulu* are the sheer number of up-sell and add-on services they offer, which appear to be geared towards taking advantage of authors.

BookBaby has an easy to use website and is up front about the services they offer. Like their eBook services, they make it clear what their basic package services are up front. They do have add-on services, but when navigating through their site, those up-sell items aren't nearly as blatant and in your face. They also charge for updates to books, but, if you are looking for quality editing and formatting services that can add value, they might be one of the distributors to consider.

The second group are two of the far more DIY and far more "free" distribution options.

- *IngramSpark*
- *D2D Print*

IngramSpark is, in my experience and opinion, by far, the best way for an author to get their POD book out into the broadest market for English language books.

They are an author-friendly front end to *Ingram Lightning Source,* which is the POD service that I started using back in 2004 when I self-published my first book. *Lightning Source* is mostly used by larger publishers and is more challenging to navigate. *IngramSpark* was created to offer a more user-friendly DIY option for self-published and independent authors, and does include options for services

They have a minimal set-up fee charge per book, and, while they have templates to assist with the creation of your POD book's interior and cover design files, most of the heavy lifting is expected to be done by you in providing print-ready PDF files.

Because Ingram is the world's largest wholesaler, having a book listed in their catalog offers authors the most extensive English language reach into the bookstore and library market available.

If you are looking for the most options in terms of trim sizes (the dimensions of the book, such as 6" X 9" or 5.5" X 8"), as well as format (trade paperback, hardcover, and even large print), then *IngramSpark* will serve those needs effectively. In addition, the discount you offer to bookstores can be controlled, and you can set a discount of up to 55% to the downstream retail channels, which does make your POD title more appealing to many retailers. (Just a reminder that Amazon *KDP Print* doesn't allow discount control in their extended distribution, and thus offers bookstores a "short" 20% discount).

With *IngramSpark* you are required to have an ISBN for each edition of your book. There are options to buy them, at a discount, via Bowker, but an ISBN will typically cost more than the setup fee for your print books themselves. (Canadians take note. Library and Archives Canada allows Canadian authors access to ISBNs for free).

Draft2Digital Print, on the other hand, is free for authors. Free title setup, free ISBN (if required), free conversion from Microsoft Word into interior print-ready PDF files, free cover flat PDF creation based on your high resolution front cover image that you might have for your eBook, and free distribution.

At the time of this writing, D2D Print is still in beta release, and is expected to be in full operation by mid 2020.

Operated through *Draft2Digital*, a leading American eBook distribution platform, *D2D Print* allows an author to set up and distribute their POD book for free. Partnering with IPG (Independent Publishers Group), a worldwide distribution distributor for independent publishers (ie, smaller publishers that include regional publishers, academic publishers that primarily use Offset printing and warehouse storage), those POD books are also made available through the same channels that appear via Ingram. With it, you will get about 98% of the distribution options you get with Ingram.

Also, the trim size choices via *D2D Print* is limited to a short list of options, rather than *IngramSpark's* more extensive offering. The format, currently, is limited to trade paperback. No hardcover options exist. The discount, while a full trade discount of 40% to bookstores, isn't something an author can edit. Nor can the author choose their distribution options. The books go to Amazon and, via IPG, through Ingram.

For a beginning author who is trying to limit their expenses and overhead but get the widest possible reach for their POD books, *D2D Print* offers exactly what they need. It can be done without having to hire a designer for the interior POD or cover files, and also comes with the convenience of using a single distributor for both eBook and POD control.

In summary, *IngramSpark* offers the widest options, widest control, but *D2D Print* offers the lowest cost setup, and, perhaps, the most user-friendly step by step process that can easily take an author from a Word manuscript and a front cover image to a print-ready POD book.

How Distribution to Bookstores Works

Before getting into the process of contacting and working with bookstores, I thought it would be important for an author to understand how bookstores list, order, receive, and shelve/stock eBooks, print books, and audiobooks.

eBooks

Let's start with eBooks, since they are perhaps the easiest to understand. Unlike print books, eBooks do not need to take up physical space, nor be stocked and purchased by a bookstore.

In order to be available for customers to purchase, it is as simple as having a book listed in an online retailer's catalog.

The eBook revolution created a significant paradigm shift in the publishing industry. No longer was an author dependent upon the multiple layers of gatekeepers (the agent, the publisher, the sales team, the bookstore buyer) in order to see their book available through bookstores. But, with that opportunity, came a new challenge. Just being listed isn't enough. And each retailer comes with their own quirks and perks, their own modus operandi.

As we have explored, an author can publish direct to all of the major online retailers (Kindle, Apple Books, Kobo, Nook, and Google Play), or they can use a third party distributor to publish their books.

Kobo is a unique retailer in that, when you have your eBook listed at Kobo, it will also be listed with dozens of their own retail partners. Kobo powers the eBook offering from retailers such as Chapters/Indigo in Canada, WHSmith in the UK, FNAC in France, Mondadori in Italy, BOL.com in the Netherlands, and the American Booksellers Association (Independent Bookstores) in the US. Customers who purchase eBooks via these retailers are still considered customers of that retailer, and, in most cases, Kobo is merely providing the content, with the customer remaining a loyal customer who is supporting their bookstore.

This distinction is important to remember when we later look at reaching out to bookstores in relation to your digital books.

While the publishing of eBooks is open and very DIY, it is important for an author to remember that it is at the discretion of each online retailer whether or not they choose to list certain titles.

Some retailers will shy away from particular genres or styles of books (many have filters on erotica, choosing to prefer romance with erotic elements rather than straight-out erotica), and some might be speciality shops. A store that specializes in Fantasy and Science-Fiction is not likely to stock mysteries and thrillers or cookbooks. A Christian bookstore is very likely to carry sweet romance, and very specific sub-genres of contemporary and historical fiction, but not carry other genres. A children's bookstore is likely to only carry titles geared toward younger readers, and perhaps a few targeted to parents.

Some authors consider such filtering done by bookstores as censorship. It is not. Censorship would be the systematic prevention of the publication and distribution of such titles. If a bookstore determines that it does not want to carry or list a specific type of book, it has every right to operate in that manner.

The way that eBook distribution works is that the bookstore lists the books, customers can purchase those books, and that eBook is delivered to the customer via the bookstore's digital reading platform options.

Taxes are collected by the bookstore and paid to the respective governments, the publisher/author share of the book is then paid out (either direct to the publisher/author, or via the distributor that publisher/author uses).

There is no overhead in terms of inventory, and the supply is unlimited.

Digital Audiobooks

I titled this section digital audiobooks rather than audiobooks, because audiobooks continue to be produced in physical form such as CD, cassette, and other formats. Those are distributed via the same channels as print, so there's no need to cover them here.

However, for digital audiobooks, the process is similar to what we just looked at with eBooks. Authors and publishers can load their audiobooks direct to retailers in some cases (For example, in the later summer of 2019

Kobo Writing Life recently launched a direct audiobook upload option) or use a third-party distribution platform. The listing appears via the online retailer website, there is no overhead or needing to stock titles, and the supply is unlimited.

Print

Print is where the real nuances of legacy publishing occur. And it is an area that traditional publishers have been navigating successfully for several dozen decades.

The advent of online bookselling significantly changed the physical book landscape since Amazon first opened as an online bookstore in July 1995. Since then, online catalogs where books could be shipped from remote warehouses on the outskirts of a city, rather than from a high rent, limited square footage retail space in a city's downtown core, or via POD technology, have grown. Most major book retailers (Barnes & Noble, Indigo Books and Music, Inc, WHSmith) have far larger title listings online than could ever appear in their stores.

Recent annual book industry statistics reveal that about half of all book sales come from online catalogs versus brick and mortar retail. That makes sense, particularly when you consider the limits of a physical location versus the virtually infinite limits of an online catalog of titles that are only printed and shipped after the book is ordered.

But what we'll be focusing on here is the process by which physical books get listed, ordered, stocked, and even returned, via physical bookstores.

And, just for the record, I am over-simplifying the process to give you an idea of how it works, rather than outlining every single nuance.

The 12 Step Life Cycle of a Print Book

One. First, the book has to be listed as available to the bookstore. That usually comes from a push data feed to a master bookstore ordering system or via an online listing accessible by the bookstore from a publisher or wholesaler. This metadata includes price, discount, format, and availability for each book. That information might come via manual data input conducted by the publisher or even the bookstore in the case of independent operations.

Two. The book is pitched or "sold" to the bookstore via a sales meeting from the publisher or a third-party sales rep. It is often still done using printed catalogs within a four-season selling cycle. It is done through telephone, online video, and in person sales calls. And the selling of a title usually occurs at least three to six months prior to the book's release. Print catalogs are produced and mailed or given to booksellers and ARCs (Advance Reader Copies) are also sometimes provided to bookstores.

This activity is one of the core reasons why a book fair like Book Expo America, which happens at the end of May each year, exists. The show was designed so that publishers could showcase their late summer and fall season titles to bookstores in the hopes of getting orders for the book industry's biggest selling period of the year: September to December.

When I was a bookstore buyer, there were periods of time where I would be meeting, often back to back, with a number of different sales reps from various publishers, flipping through catalogs, looking at performance of past titles, and determining which handful of titles from the hundreds they had available, I might order to stock in my store.

Three. Someone within that bookstore operation has to perform some sort of curation step to make the book visible or available for physical distribution or acquisition to the bookstore. It is also assigned an appropriate merchandising category, usually adapted from the suggested category provided by the publisher.

At this point, the book moves into the "stocked by bookstore" segments of its life cycle.

Four. The book is ordered for the bookstore, either directly from the publisher or via a third-party wholesaler.

Five. The book is shipped by the publisher/wholesaler and received into the bookstore's physical stock.

Six. The book is shelved or merchandised in the assigned location in the bookstore.

Seven. The book remains in stock for an indeterminable period with the intention that a consumer picks it off the shelf, or a bookseller recommends it to a customer, and a purchase is made. The reason I use "indeterminable" is because the time period varies based on either the store or the merchandising category the book is listed in. Some sections, where space is limited and the title selection is high, have shorter windows, compared to other categories where space isn't at as much of a premium.

In this part of a book's life cycle, it is typically known as a frontlist title. Publishers put a lot of their emphasis from their sales and marketing department on frontlist titles, but that focus is usually only for a limited number of weeks for the book's release. Because, particularly in the case of larger publishers, there is always an influx of new titles coming, so there is a revolving focus.

Depending on the publisher or bookseller, a book moves from being considered a frontlist title to a backlist title after a specific period after its release date which can be anywhere from six months to one year.

Eight. Once the pre-determined "shelf-life" of the book is reached, a decision is made, usually via a system-generated report, to pull the book from stock, transfer it to the bookstore's shipping and receiving department, and box it up and return it to the wholesaler or publisher warehouse for a credit.

And herein lies the rub for traditional publishing. Returns.

Within traditional publishing and bookselling, if a book that is stocked in stores doesn't sell, it is returned to the publisher for a refund/credit to the store.

And this leads to the ninth step, the beginning of what I like to consider the potential "afterlife" of a book.

Nine. Depending on the title in its particular life cycle, since warehouse space is limited, the publisher decides if it wants to keep the book as active and in-print, in the hopes it will be popular and ordered again.

This might occur if a movie or television series is made from a book, or an "act of Oprah" happens – an old bookseller phrase meaning that some popular culture recommendation occurred, raising the book up and out of obscurity.

It is also possible that if the book has "staying power" it is considered a core title for most bookstores. A core title is a somewhat "evergreen" title, and one that most bookstores usually always have in stock. Think of a book you would expect to find in almost any bookstore you walk into, regardless of how long it has been out or the season. This would be books like Steven Covey's *The Seven Habits of Highly Effective People*, Jane Austin's *Pride and Prejudice*, Harper Lee's *To Kill A Mockingbird*, William Shakespeare's *Hamlet*, Charles Darwin's *On the Origin of Species*, an Oxford or Webster dictionary. It could also be a title that is not universal, but which is considered "core" for a themed or genre specific bookstore. Science Fiction classics such as Frank Herbert's *Dune* or Isaac Asimov's *Foundation* in a sci-fi shop, specific bibles in a religious bookstore, etc.

If the publisher determines that the book is "dead" then a decision is made to either pulp and destroy it or make it available for being remaindered.

Ten. This is the death of a book, or its resurrection back into the book trade supply chain.

Remaindering is a way for the publisher to liquidate their returned or unsold inventory of a title, selling it either to a bookstore or to a remainder wholesaler non-returnable at greatly reduced prices. A $25.00 Hardcover, for example, with 10,000 copies sitting in warehouse stock, might be remaindered for $1.00 per unit, allowing the publisher to recoup $10,000 of their original investment, providing a cash flow for operations, but also freeing up inventory warehouse space.

That remaindered title might be sold as non-returnable from that remainder wholesaler to bookstores for $2.00, and, in return, priced at $4.99 to $6.99 by the bookstore. Remainders are often placed on tables or other displays at the front of the bookstore. They are often the highest margin product in a bookstore, with the bookstore earning 50% to 80%, instead of the regular 40% to 50% they receive on regular trade books.

Because bookstores buy remaindered titles at a significant discount, they either continue to further discount the title until it sells out, or they decide to do their own pulping of it, losing the least amount of money on that investment.

Returns: A Major Side-Effect of Traditional Publishing and Bookselling

Returns have long been a consistent and constant challenge in the book publishing industry, because they allow retail bookstores to take casual risks on books that either have uncertain demand or have not yet proven to sell. Returns represent a significant cost, perhaps the largest uncontrollable cost, for publishers.

In an industry where returns are the norm, the publisher holds the majority of the risk.

Returns have been a regular part of the publishing industry in North America since the 1930s, near the time of the Great Depression. This "consignment" style of retail is the result of a tactic that publishers employed as a temporary strategy, while times were tough, to overcome the hesitation and wariness that booksellers had on investing in ordering books, titles, and authors that they weren't 100% sure about. It became a "guarantee" style system that, if the book didn't sell, the bookseller could return it for a full credit.

In his 1988 book, *This Business of Publishing: An Insider's View of Current Trends and Tactics*, by Allworth Press, Richard Curtis described the system as "grossly inefficient, wasteful, costly, and risky." He went on to say that in its worst manifestations, it is quite close to fraudulent.

The norm of the returns process has become an industry standard that booksellers and publishers both rely on, while also abhorring.

Publishers regularly overprint, because if they don't have enough inventory to meet demand, it results in a potential decrease in the bookseller interest and orders while they reprint and restock.

In the same vein, bookstores might default to overbuy, for the fear of being out of stock and losing front line sales.

Returns aren't a one-way problem. They do cause issues to both players. Publishers pay the costs for shipping to bookstores; but bookstores, pay for staff labor to pick, pack, and ship the books back. When I started working in the book industry in 1992, there was ongoing talk about why this is something that should stop. And I am aware that talk had been going on long before I set foot in the industry.

The Main Difference Between Print on Demand (POD) and Offset Print Distribution

Again, I am simplifying the overview of printing types, and dividing them into two main categories for the purpose of offering a high-level understanding of this business.

Those two categories are Offset and Digital printing.

Offset printing, which originated in the 1870s, but is derived from "moveable type" impression printing and Gutenberg's 1439 printing press, is a commonly used printing technique in which an inked image is transferred from an etched "plate" (metal or otherwise) to the printing surface. The setup for Offset printing is typically more time consuming and expensive and works best for larger print runs. Amortized over larger print runs, Offset printing can result in one of the most inexpensive print per unit costs available.

Digital printing uses electrostatic rollers (also known as "drums") to apply ink toner onto paper. The toner is usually applied to the paper using intense heat. Digital printing can easily and quickly produce a single sheet of paper. Think about your home or office printer or photocopier. Print on Demand (POD) operations are a type of digital printing. While the price of a digital print on demand title starts off low, that cost typically doesn't become lower with larger print runs the same way it does for Offset printing.

Offset printing makes the most economic sense for larger print runs (typically 500 copies or more, although this number differs depending on the book's page count and trim size). Digital printing is best for shorter print runs (under 500 copies), and even one-off printing. Such as print on demand.

Large publishing operations likely employ a combination of both printing techniques. Because Offset printing takes a long time, if a book that was originally created via Offset printing runs out of stock due to huge consumer demand and popularity, a publisher might use Digital printing for quick turn-around to fulfill immediate orders so as not to loose out on sales while the book is out of stock, and the longer-term Offset printing for the next print run is being produced.

Offset printing doesn't necessarily mean returnable, just like Digital printing doesn't necessarily mean non-returnable.

Returnability is usually based on the actual print run itself and whether or not the title will be stocked in a distribution warehouse.

For most authors who are taking the DIY approach, Digital printing is the most common option, where there is no warehouse inventory, and titles are printed and shipped only after an order is placed (either via a bookstore, or a direct from consumer purchase that comes from an online retailer).

And typically, most of an independently or self-published author's books are likely to be non-returnable to bookstores.

Considering the legacy lifecycle of a book that we just looked at, this makes most indie author titles outliers within the standard process.

But that doesn't mean an indie author can't still work within that system.

In the next section, we'll take a look at working with various bookstores.

Working with Bookstores

Working with Online Bookstores: eBooks

This section is going to cover a high overview of some of the highlights to consider when working with the major English language online retailers. Each has its own unique approach and nuances, but regardless of which one you are looking at, it's important to remember this: your professional behavior, approach, and communication when working within their systems and interacting with them should always be a foregone conclusion.

Amazon – Amazon Kindle

Countless numbers of books exist on how to succeed on Amazon. Considering they are the world's biggest bookstore, and often represent the majority of sales within the indie author community, that makes sense. So I won't go into too much depth here. In the resource section of this book I will list a few helpful and insightful books about Amazon from authors who know it far better than I do.

Let's first start off with something that is not only useful, but also extremely important regardless of how you publish: *Author Central.*

With *Author Central,* a free account you can create at Amazon, you can set up an author profile that appears on

Amazon for your print, audio, and eBooks. At its basic function, you can claim the books where you are the primary author or are a contributing author (in the case of anthologies, etc) regardless of whether it is a traditionally published or self-published book, load an author profile photo, a biography, additional photos and videos, a link to automatically import posts from your blog.

If you have an author profile set up, when someone clicks on your author name when looking at a title on Amazon, instead of returning a string of search results for your name, it brings the customer to your specific author landing page. This is important, because, instead of the consumer seeing a barrage of other titles from other authors and publishers, they are looking only at you and your books. It provides a bit of focus.

At the higher level, *Author Central* allows you to add editorial reviews (reviews from journals, newspapers and other sources) to a book's listing, track and analyse your sales rank by book, author, and within NPD (formerly Neilson) BookScan data for the United States. It also allows you to easily see all the customer reviews that have been added to your books.

Author Central appears not only for Amazon.com in the US, but also in the UK, France, Germany, and Japan. In order to have an author landing page for each of these territories, you'll need to set up separate accounts. I would recommend that, at the very least you set up both a US (.com) and UK (.co.uk) *Author Central* account to ensure that, in the English language territories, you have that advantage.

Unlike most of the other online retailers, Amazon is based heavily on algorithms and recommendations personalized specifically to each unique customer, rather than manual merchandising by bookseller personnel. Amazon has never shared how their algorithms work, and almost every week, someone writes an article about how the algorithms have changed. There are numerous books that explain them. And, the minute someone seems to figure them out, they change again. Chasing algorithms is like a game of smoke and mirrors. The only one thing I can be sure of is that relying on something that is almost guaranteed to keep changing and evolving is a risky dependency.

One thing that hasn't seemed to change, at least in the more than ten years I've been attending to this, is the fact that Amazon rewards relevancy over time. If there is a consistent pattern of activity and interest in a particular book, that book is more likely to surface to more of the right customers. So, at the high level, any long-term strategy that works toward consistent interest in your book over time (searches, clicks, purchases, previews, free downloads, Kindle Unlimited page reads) is likely to be more rewarding than single intense spikes that peters off immediately.

At the time of this writing, running Amazon Advertising Ads (which, unfortunately, can only be run on titles that you are publishing direct to Amazon), is one way to help increase some of those things, by paying to get your book in front of more of the right people in your target audience.

It is, of course, very much a pay-to-play system that requires ongoing dedication and commitment of time and up-front cash.

But, like many other things related to Amazon, entire books have been written about it, and by folks with far more insights, perspective, and knowledge about the intricacies of Amazon than me. In the resource section at the end of this book, I list some of the many books and online links to helpful articles in this area.

In terms of a personal relationship with Amazon, it's mostly a case of, if you're a big enough author, Amazon will reach out to you. Once you are selling enough, Amazon will assign you a personal rep. Of course, in their ongoing elusive ways, Amazon has never shared what "enough" is. They play their cards really close to their chests. And I imagine that "enough," much like their shifting algorithms, continue to morph and change and remain undefined, at least from the outside.

Networking with Amazon at in person events is a little like trying to hang out with the cool kids in high school. If you are popular, you're in. If you're new to the school, good luck trying to impress the cool kids.

Amazon's online customer service is typically responsive and helpful, and I have had plenty of excellent service from multiple representatives over the years. Similarly, many of their next-level services come from contacting them online via the *Help* menu within *Kindle Direct Publishing* – things like ensuring your eBook, print, and audiobook are linked on the same item page (which doesn't always happen automatically), having your book added to additional categories, or making sure there is a unique series landing page for your series books, which someone on their customer service team usually has to manually link.

But, on the flip side, I have attended dozens of in person Amazon presentations at conferences from Book Expo America, London Book Fair, Frankfurt Book Fair, Digital Book World, RWA, NINC, 20BooksVegas™, and more, and have witnessed that the content shared is no more useful than the online help text and online support they have.

At the 2019 20BooksVegas™ conference, for example, I watched Amazon reps take the main stage with seven hundred people in the audience, most of which were likely already earning monthly three, four, and five figure incomes from Amazon, and waste their time explaining how to upload and publish a book to Amazon.

There is no customization for audience, no moving off of the "script" and virtually no value in wasting your time sitting through a presentation from Amazon. You might get more value from a panel where an Amazon rep is participating, or via any opportunity to chat with an Amazon rep one on one.

Since 2011, I have also networked and hung out, chatted, and drank with Amazon representatives. They are great people, smart people, personable people. But they are also extremely reluctant to ever actually share useful information about how to leverage their system and increase sales. Almost any book or article by David Gaughran or podcast interview with Mark Dawson is likely to offer far more insight and perspective on Amazon than you will get from those interactions. Unless, of course, you're one of the cool kids.

Also, due to the sheer size of the massive company, Amazon does have a reputation for being a giant corporation with carbon-cut out responses to personal frustrations, and addressing specific questions with blanket token responses. There is a lot of "the left hand doesn't know what the right hand is doing" between regular *KDP* eBook publishing, *KDP Print*, and *Author Central*, for example.

There are likely more people who work for Amazon *KDP* than in the entire team in all of Kobo.

Authors often both simultaneously hate and love Amazon; parallels have long been drawn between Amazon and an abusive spouse that authors both love, and fear, at the same time.

Apple Books

At the time of the writing of this book, Apple's eBook offering is known as Apple Books. It used to be called iBooks but changed when Apple released iOS 12.

Unlike Amazon, which is mostly algorithm based, Apple operates under a team of merchandisers that curate titles. And they do this curation in most of the major English language territories. Sometimes they do it in conjunction, and sometimes independently.

Similar to Amazon, if you are an author who is worthy of attention, Apple will reach out to you. You will have a contact with them, but you are requested to not violate the confidence they share with you.

Apple reps are often in attendance at all of the major conferences and workshops. But they are rarely visible. I remember it took me a long time to figure out who the Apple reps were. They are brilliantly adept and elusive. I've always thought of them like ninjas, moving about in the shadows, always there, and only revealing their presence to those deemed worthy.

They appear to have a policy that prevents any of their reps from being on the same panel with, or even networking or socializing with any people who work for a competitor.

I worked at a University Bookstore for years and our computer department was an authorized Apple store. The contract for that seemed to be as thick as a city phone book, filled with a seemingly endless lists of rules, guidelines, restrictions, policies related to operations, merchandising, etc. So, it wouldn't surprise me if the company would have similar operational procedures for their staff.

But they are good people. Extremely good people. I actually adore all of the folks at Apple that I've had the pleasure of interacting with; this only happened once I left Kobo in 2017, of course, because, prior to that, my interactions were extremely short and limited to a polite hand-shake or friendly nod.

One of the many things I admire and respect about Apple is that they don't seem to be hung up on whether or not you are publishing to Apple Books direct or you are publishing to them via a third party.

In my role at *Draft2Digital*, the Apple reps I interact with are interested in helping us promote and prop up authors and titles that could use a little bit of extra flexibility. And they aren't bothered by how the book is published to Apple Books – they just want excellent content they can merchandise and present to their customers.

There are a few things to keep in mind about Apple Books that are important.

While romance does extremely well there, they tend to shy away from titles that are more heavily erotica based, and even prefer book covers that are a little less steamy. They are more apt to default to preferring sweet romance versus romance that is more about overt sexual content. Similarly, they do like to see books from across the genres.

In additional, they are quite sensitive to whether or not an author is inclusive in their behavior. If you are looking to get a book featured in an Apple promotion and your website only mentions or links to Amazon, it suggests that you are only invested in a single retailer, and one that is not them.

Think of it from their perspective. They go out of their way to help you, and yet you are only looking at and driving people who go to your website to their main competitor. How do you think that makes them feel?

This perspective is something that will be pervasive for all other retailers that aren't Amazon. So do keep that in mind.

Google – Google Play

Google, like Amazon and Apple, is one of the largest technology powerhouse companies in the digital world. But their track record within the eBook game has been inconsistent at best.

Until very recently, Google seemed to have shut their doors to indie authored titles, only reaching out directly to authors who already had a proven track record of sales in other eBook marketplaces. I have met perhaps a dozen authors in the past ten years whose sales via Google Play eBooks is high, second only to their Amazon Kindle sales. So it's not a market to be ignored.

It has just been a difficult market to get into.

One of the best ways to get your books into Google would have been through a third-party distributor like *Draft2Digital* or *PublishDrive*; however, towards the end of 2019, *Draft2Digital* announced they were shutting down that offering, stating that the process Google was forcing authors to publish to their platform using a third-party was not efficient, time-saving, nor a scalable long-term solution.

However, toward the end of the drafting of this book, I had the opportunity to meet with Google representatives who appeared at the November 2019 20BooksVegas™ conference in Las Vegas, Nevada. They appeared on a panel discussing wide publishing and made themselves available to speak one on one with authors, indicating, in a very positive fashion, that they would be back in the game in full swing come January 2020.

I have high hopes that Google will be the first major digital player to actually interact with and engage with the author community and could very well make them the real contender with Amazon Kindle in the eBook market that the world needs.

I am keeping my fingers crossed and, as updated information about this comes in, I will post updates to this at www.markleslie.ca/authorsbookstoreslibraries.

In the meantime, remember that, like the approach discussed for Apple Books, make sure you are including a link to Google on your author website and in social media, and not just pointing only to Amazon.

Kobo

From the very beginning, Kobo, the Canadian-born answer to Kindle, has always been an approachable company. The company's CEO, Michael Tamblyn, has long been an engaged figure within the Canadian and international publishing scene, and is as likely to mingle with authors as any of the other members of this company. The same goes for the *Kobo Writing Life* team.

I should pause to admit that I come with a huge bias towards this company and this team, as I worked there for six years (2011 to 2017), and was behind the creation of *Kobo Writing Life*, their direct to Kobo self-publishing platform. And I am proud that the team has continued in my example of being directly and intimately engaged in the author community.

So, do remember to take all my positivity with a grain of salt.

When Kobo representatives (regardless of whether they are Kobo general or from the *Kobo Writing Life* team), are presenting at a conference, or on a panel, they are quite transparent and willing to share in depth details and insights. If you get the opportunity to network and meet with them in person, either at a conference, or when they host their frequent open houses at their Toronto, Ontario head office location, do take advantage of that.

When you email the team, you'll get a response directly from one of the dozen or so people who work directly on the team, and not from some out-sourced customer service group.

If you do have a direct *Kobo Writing Life* account, make sure to request the promotions tab. There are multiple promotions running every month; in my experience, the free spotlight (for perma-free titles), and the monthly 30% or 40% off promotions tend to work best for gaining your book traction.

The majority of promotional opportunities will come to those who use *Kobo Writing Life* to publish direct. Kobo plays a strong and very blatant favorable bias towards those authors.

They run a podcast and a blog and are constantly looking for great content. Articles about the craft or business of writing are enjoyed, so emailing them and pitching them an idea for a guest article or guest appearance on their podcast helps make you memorable to them. When doing this, please be sure that your pitch is one that is meant to help other authors; the promotion or mention of you and your books should be secondary, or a mere whisper in terms of the overall content being pitched.

Kobo, like Apple, and the other retailers, is extremely sensitive to whether or not authors are inclusive about their book links on their websites and in social media. Make sure to include mention of Kobo (with the correct logo – they have changed theirs half a dozen times in as many years) and not just talk about Amazon.

I could go on for over 200 pages about working with and leveraging Kobo. In fact, I have. In another book. So, rather than repeat myself here, I'll suggest you consider checking out my 2018 book **Killing It on Kobo**, or, for free, the dozens of hours of podcast interviews where I've shared the same information. Links appear at www.markleslie.ca/authorsbookstoreslibraries.

Nook

Nook is the eBook brand for Barnes and Noble, the largest chain retailer in the United States. The Nook eBook reading devices are available for purchase in their big box stores across the US as well as online. Like Google Play, Nook has been inconsistent over the years, with numerous changes to personnel and processes for working with them, and like Apple, the brand by which they operate has also changed names multiple times.

Nook favors working directly with them via *B&N Press*, the current incarnation of their direct publishing platform, and offer promotions only to authors who are publishing direct.

I have met with some very wonderful, intelligent, and passionate people from the Nook eBook publishing team over the years, and they have always been open to speaking directly to authors and working with them. They have been personable and willing to answer hard questions. I both like and admire them.

Their online response to emails is consistent, and, meeting their representatives in person is most definitely always a pleasant and solid experience.

However, my instinct or gut steers me in a different direction. At one time in their recent history, the direct to Nook self-publishing team was working with an arm of *Author Solutions*, a company that I consistently recommend authors avoid, due to their less than transparent business practices. So far as I know, that relationship has ended, but it still gives me a bit of a sour feeling.

Considering their history, the instability of the direct publishing platform, and the overall insolvency of the company in recent years (In 2019 Barnes and Noble was taken over by a company that, in the UK, sold-off the eBook arm of their business), I worry about suggesting that authors invest too much of their time and energy in publishing direct; it might just be work that an author has to re-do all that work.

And, regardless of whether you publish direct or use a third-party distributor to publish your eBooks to Nook, as mentioned with all of the non-Amazon retailers above, take note to include links to and mentions of Nook on your author website and social media. Nook, like the others, is sensitive to the inclusiveness.

Smashwords

While *Smashwords* is often seen as a third-party distributor, it is important for authors to remember that it is also a bookstore that sells direct to consumers. While the browsing and shopping experience is a far cry from the smooth shopping experience one gets on Amazon, *Smashwords* is available to a much broader global market.

The team at *Smashwords*, lead by Mark Coker, a true pioneer in the overall self-publishing and indie-publishing revolution, are small, and are all really good folks. I've had the privilege of getting to know Mark and many of his team members over the years and admire that they have long been the champions of the indie author.

Among the opportunities you have working direct with *Smashwords* are the occasional seasonal promotions that are offered to *Smashwords* authors and the DIY promotions codes and tools. Within the *Smashwords* Dashboard, under *Marketing Tools*, you'll see a Coupon Manager. This allows you to assign coupon codes to eBooks, which you can then share with customers on your email list, press releases, or via your blog social networks. Customers can enter the code prior to completing their checkout at Smashwords.com to receive the allotted discount. They can then download the eBook in ePub, mobi, or any other formats you choose to make available.

There are additional reader/customer insights that come from *Smashwords*, such as being able to see and track who has "Favorited" you as an author, complete with their social media handles, and even website, if they entered it, and how many people from which countries have signed up for your author updates.

The Importance of Being Inclusive

I know that I harped on it with virtually every single retailer that I just went through, but it stands repeating. The reason it stands repeating is that, despite having told this to authors repeatedly over the years, it is something that is quickly and easily forgotten. And I get it. Amazon is the world's biggest bookstore. So the term "Kindle" comes to mind first. Authors are also obsessed with their Amazon ranking, and often seek to drive all traffic there in order to elevate themselves on that platform.

But too often it happens at the expense of the other platforms. And they are paying attention; they are aware. And every time you are "all Amazon all the time" it's a huge slap in the face to them.

That's not necessarily, the best way to stay in their good graces.

Find and follow the various retailers and their direct self-publishing platforms online. "At" them in your social media posts, with inclusive links. When your book is newly launched to or is ranking high on their platform, share that, share screen shots, let them know you're excited and aware of your book on their platform, and publicly acknowledge and thank readers on those platforms.

A little bit of acknowledgement goes a long way.

And, for Pete's sake, if you're lucky enough to get any sort of promotion at or to a retailer, share it and ensure they know you are sharing it.

Universal Book Links

One of the best ways to easily ensure that you are using inclusive links it to take advantage of some of the tools that allow you a single link that includes all the retailers.

Books2Read.com is one I recommend.

Any book you publish through *Draft2Digital* will automatically get a Books2Read universal book link. But you can create a universal book link for any book, regardless of how it is published. And the tool is free.

It not only can automatically crawl and pull in links to retailers from all over the world, but it also uses geo-targeting to ensure the consumer gets to the correct location of the website. (For example, Amazon, Apple, and Kobo all have multiple versions of their websites for different global territories that display different default prices.)

When a consumer/reader clicks on a Books2Read link they see the book cover, title and author for the book, plus a link to all of the retailers the book is on (using the most up to date authorized versions of each retailer's logo). When that reader clicks on a specific retailer icon, it will take them to that eBook's landing page there. It will also offer a pop-up that asks the consumer if they'd like to set that retailer as their default store. If they do, the next time they follow any Books2Read link for any other book, it will automatically take them directly to that store.

Using a universal single link to all retailers can save you time from having to manage dozens of different links for every single book and in the back of every single book that you publish.

Notes on Using Third Party Distributors

If you use a third-party distributor to publish your eBook to any of the retail platforms, such as *Draft2Digital*, *Smashwords*, *PublishDrive*, or *StreetLib*, do be aware that there are promotional opportunities available. If you are unfamiliar with the opportunities that exist, contact the support or help contacts of the platform and ask them. The promotional opportunities are likely not to be as good as what you might get when you are publishing direct, but the benefit to you might be managing your eBook via a single platform.

I know from personal experience, that *Draft2Digital* works hard at finding ways to spotlight and promote forthcoming titles to downstream retailers as well as collaborating with the platforms to get those titles into ongoing promotions.

At the time of this writing, Apple is the one retailer that isn't wanting to force authors to publish direct, as has been more open to offering authors promotional space regardless of how they publish. I can't say the same for Kobo or Nook.

Your OWN Bookstore

Since we are talking about working with online bookstores for eBooks, I thought I should pause to ensure you are aware that you can also include your own store, managed from your own website.

Companies such as BookFunnel allow for authors to sell their own books on their own websites using Payhip, PayPal, Selz, Shopify, or WooCommerce. When the integrated transaction completes, BookFunnel will email a private download link to the buyer automatically. And, as it is part of their service offering, if a reader has any trouble transferring a book to their reading device, the top-notch support team at BookFunnel is always happy to assist, ensuring that you, the author, never need to worry about that tech support.

This type of direct selling is important to understand, because, with your own bookstore, you can generate your own unique coupon codes at any time, and engage in promotions that you are in control of.

Working with Online Bookstores: Print Books

If you are traditionally published, your publisher has likely already taken care of listing your book with every major online bookstore channel, even if they are using POD instead of Offset printing.

If you publish your POD book direct to Amazon via *KDP Print*, the book will be listed at Amazon. If you publish your POD book via *B&N Press*, it will appear on Barnes and Noble.

When you publish your POD book wide to all the platforms using *IngramSpark, D2D Print,* or another POD provider, your book will automatically be listed at

Amazon, Barnes and Noble, Chapters/Indigo, WHSmith and hundreds of other online bookstores.

Apart from the platforms that offer direct publishing (Amazon and Barnes and Noble), there aren't many opportunities for promotions. However, via Amazon Advertising and some specific *B&N Press* promotions, there are opportunities to work those systems for additional traction.

In most cases, the eBook and the print book will be listed together. If you self published eBook and print through KDP the listing should happen automatically. But if they don't, you can contact Amazon through the Help menu and request that they link them. And at Kobo, for example, when you enter your eBook you have the option of entering the primary print ISBN. Kobo doesn't sell print books, but Kobo uses this field when submitting eBook data to their publishing partners around the world, such as Indigo Books & Music, Inc in Canada. That data can be used to automatically link the print and eBook editions of the book, helping that title's cross-over sales potential.

Considering that online bookstores have existed since the mid 1990s I'm surprised that someone somewhere hasn't used technology to host some sort of virtual event featuring an author and pre-signed books ready to be shipped out. Maybe the hassle and work would be too much work for too little return on investment. Or maybe it has been done, just not effectively enough for the idea to spread.

But it's important to remember that, in the strictly online world for print books, the opportunity for direct relationships is extremely limited.

Working with Online Bookstores: Audiobooks

If you are traditionally published your publisher has most likely already made your physically produced audiobook available via the regular print channels, or the digital audiobook available to either Audible and Apple, or to all of the retailers.

If you are publishing through ACX your audiobook will be available only at Audible and via Apple. Or, if your audiobook was acquired by Audible as an exclusive (similar to a traditional publishing deal, but with a mandate for Amazon and Audible exclusivity), then that is likely to come with a built-in relationship with people at Audible and the potential for promotional consideration.

Regardless of how you publish, Audible, one of the largest players in the market, does have an *Audible Author Profile* which is a landing page featuring your author photo and bio, which is pulled from the information you have entered in your Amazon *Author Central* account.

In the spring of 2019, BookBub announced a new promotional audiobook platform called *Chirp*. All titles available to chirp are fed through Findaway, the audiobook production company. So, if your publisher has made your audiobook available to Findaway, it should be listed there. Or, if you use *Findaway Voices* to self-publish your audiobook, it will also be listed there.

If, however, your audiobook is published as exclusive to Audible via ACX, then it won't appear in *Chirp*.

Apart from *Chirp* and a small handful of audiobook promotion platforms, there aren't many marketing opportunities for audiobooks at this moment in publishing; but more are likely to emerge as it continues to grow.

And, similarly, with the exception of the *Kobo Writing Life* team, who started accepting audiobooks directly through their self-publishing platform in the summer of 2019, there aren't many opportunities to have contact directly with audiobook retailers.

But, where you can have contact, make sure that the retailer knows the relationship between the audiobook and the other formats. On Kobo it's a manual link setup that you'll have to email the team about via *writinglife@kobo.com*. On Amazon it is usually automatic but using the Help menu to request linking the audiobook helps.

The reason I suggest it's important to have the audiobook linked is that any promotional or merchandising that happens for your eBook or print book will also have a halo effect on the visibility and sales of your audiobook. It's not uncommon for an eBook that is being featured via a BookBub email blast, for example, to come with a side-effect of an increase in audiobook sales. Some customers, happening upon the great deal, are intrigued by the title, but might prefer to grab the book in audio.

Working with Brick-and-Mortar Bookstores

Brick-and-Mortar bookstores are mostly going to be concerned with print books. Although this might include physical formats of audiobooks such as CDs, cassettes, etc.

Regardless of whether or not the bookstore is an independent one or a chain bookstore, their expectations about print books are not all that different. As discussed in the pervious section about print, both types expect your book to be returnable and to have a trade discount, which is usually at least 40%.

If readers are not allowed to return your book, and if bookstores aren't allowed to return the book back to the publisher or wholesaler, stores aren't as likely to take the risk of ordering it and stocking it on their shelves. You must also offer a trade discount to the store.

Another consistent between the two is that the bookstores expect your book to appeal to their customers enough to make a purchase. It must be something they believe will sell to their customers. At the end of the day, these retail operations have to pay rent, utilities, and labor costs in order to remain in operation. As beautiful and delightful a bookstore (that room filled with books) can be, it's still, fundamentally, a retail business.

I have overseen inventory for both a chain bookstore and an independent bookstore and I could only afford to keep in stock books that actually "turned-over" on a regular basis. A book taking up space on a shelf for years was merely collecting dust and not earning money. If a book didn't earn its space on a shelf, it would be returned and something new would be brought in. There is always something new available, and the shelf space can be quite precious.

But let's now dip into some of the differences between the different types of bookstores.

Chain Bookstores

A chain bookstore is one that has multiple locations and usually has a separate and remote home office where head office executives and staff manage the procedural operations and policies. Often, buyers operate out of the home office location. Although, in the case of some chains, buyers might actually be situated in a location, a flagship store, or a buyer for a particular genre might be located in a store that offers that speciality; regional buyers might also be in operation in the case of larger chains.

In terms of major English language market chains, here are examples of just a few of them:

- Australia
  - Angus & Robertson

- Borders
- Collins Booksellers
- The Co-op Bookshop
- Dymocks Booksellers
- Koorong
- QBD (Queensland Book Depot)
- Canada
  - Archambault
  - Indigo Books & Music Inc
  - Renaud-Bray
- New Zealand
  - Borders
  - Dymocks Booksellers
  - Paper Plus
  - Whitcoulls
- United Kingdom
  - Blackwell's
  - Foyles
  - WH Smith
  - Waterstones
  - The Works
  - Daunt Books
- United States
  - Barnes & Noble
  - Bookmans
  - Books-A-Million
  - Seagull Book
  - Follett's
  - Half Price Books
  - Hudson News

Canada has a couple of independent chain bookstores such as Book City and McNally Robinson. The United States also has some major independent chains, such as Powell's Books, Scheler Books & Music, Joseph-Beth Booksellers, David-Kidd Booksellers, and Tattered Cover.

Though these are all technically chain stores, their operation is more akin what you would expect when looking at or dealing with an independent store.

In addition, other major chains, such as Walmart and Target, also have book sections. Their selection of titles is often extremely limited and their in stock listing sticks merely to the most popular top-selling and seasonal titles.

Bookstore chains such as Barnes & Noble often create consistent layout and merchandising experiences for each of their stores; the idea is that a customer visiting one should feel "at home" or "familiar" with them regardless of what city or state they are in. Most of their frontlist buying decisions happen at a corporate level and many of their in-store marketing signs and displays are all about global branding that is decided centrally and communicated out to the stores.

There is often regional and local opportunity for management and staff of these stores to top-up or round-out buying. And different chains and stores will have implemented their own unique processes for acquiring titles outside of the head office buyers methodologies and strategies, but which also have to fall in line with home office dictated standards.

Consider how commercial your book and its branding are when you approach chain stores and appeal to them from that perspective.

In order to understand some of the nuances about chain bookstores, I thought it might be best for me to share an example from my own experience when I managed the product database for Indigo Books & Music, Inc. (AKA Chapters/Indigo) in Canada.

Publishers and wholesalers submitted their online listings via an html-based industry standard data feed known as ONIX (Online Information Exchange), or via Excel or similar flat file transmissions of data. In the early 2000's, I had been behind the creation of a manual entry system for small publishers and independent authors, known as SYME (System for Manual Entry). The intent was to collect information and metadata to allow Chapters/Indigo to have the book available for sale on their website to consumers.

All of the titles successfully imported were made available for sale on the website. But not all of those titles were listed in the internal master brick-and-mortar retail database.

A sub-set of that data was curated into the physical retail ordering catalog by a number of head-office buyers. There were between half a dozen and a dozen book buyers, each with their own slate of genres they would purchase for. The buyers would review the larger data set of titles available, either by publisher, or by querying titles by forthcoming publication date and genre. They would also meet with sales reps who would visit the Toronto head office to review stacks of catalogs with them; in addition they would take telephone sales calls from some remote sales agents; and they would also attend seasonal trade shows like Book Expo Canada (now defunct), and Book Expo America.

In addition to these sales calls and networking events, they would run, or have assistants who worked with them, run reports on their sections to indicate how they were doing overall, what titles were most popular (and which ones weren't moving or "turning" inventory as expected), which stores were performing well, and trying to incorporate all of those insights, research, and knowledge into making their ongoing seasonal buying decisions.

They would determine, for all frontlist and forthcoming titles, which books would be added to the master brick-and-mortar retail system, but also which stores would get what quantities of which titles.

The stores were all placed into grouping or categories based upon their size (square footage), location (urban downtown, urban suburbs, or rural), and overall expected annual net sales. A 22,000 square foot big-box suburban Chapters location, for example, compared with a 3,000 square foot mall store. The larger one might contain a complement of 75,000 to 100,000 unique titles, while the smaller might carry less than 10,000.

If the buyer has determined they will order 10,000 copies of a new release, they also have to determine which stores will get how many copies of each for their initial fulfillment. The aforementioned larger format location might be one of one hundred locations to each receive 50 copies. A few smaller ones, let's say fifty of them, each receive 30 copies. Twenty-five others are to receive 20 copies each; and ten others each receive 10 copies. Within the smaller format stores (the other one hundred and fifteen, it's not as simple as dividing up the remaining stock equally to about 25 units each. Some might perform better than others in that category, so distribution can vary. Some smaller stores might receive more units than a slower performing big-box store, while some locations might be allotted only 1 or 2 copies.

This is all based on complex algorithms, sales history, expected and projected sales, and, as always a little bit of "gut" feeling from the buyer based on their experience in the trade.

Once the books are ordered, the local store sometimes has the option to top-up the buyer's order. Sometimes, depending on the store and the buyer and the procedure, the top-up is authorized at the store level, or the regional level, or by the head office buyer themselves. And, more often, once the book arrives in the store, the store often has the means to request re-orders of the book so that, as the title begins to sell off the shelf, new copies can be received back into the store so that the book does not actually run down to zero stock.

In the case of another title, one that the buyer might only wish to purchase 100 to 500 copies, not every store is going to get initial stock. And in some cases, not every store is even going to be able to see and order that title for stock.

Four times a year each buyer makes this decision for thousands of titles and thousands of unique combinations and factors related to the store and the market. And, if that's not enough to complicate matters, the buyers and the company executives, might also have to navigate mandated title placement in the case of specially curated collections (Indigo, for example, has a "Heather's Picks" prominent display in every location, uniquely curated titles from Heather Reisman, the company's founder and CEO), and "co-op" deals with the major publishers. Co-op placements are paid placements for high visibility retail space in the store. It exists within all retailers, and bookstores, of course, are no exception. These co-op placements exist not just for new releases, but potentially for a major publisher imprint promotion to feature their titles, both backlist and frontlist, on an end cap, table, or display.

After all is said and done, don't forget, as I shared earlier in this chapter, ongoing reports are run to find titles that are not selling, and those titles are returned to the publishers. Backlist titles that are proven, via ongoing reports, help the chain to establish a list of what are often referred to as "core" titles for either all of their stores, or for a breakdown of stores based on their size and format. As discussed earlier in this chapter when talking about a book's life cycle, a core title is one that is a backlist (more than 6 months or a year old), that has a consistent and proven track record of sales and high ongoing customer demand.

If there is a book that has been out for more than a year and you would expect to find in stock at virtually any bookstore you walk into, that is likely to be considered a "core" title by many different book operations.

All of these things, these decisions, happen on a regular cycle to make room for the constant influx of books.

As you can see, the majority of the initial ordering and merchandising decisions happen at head office and everything is filtered top-down to the store.

But, depending on the chain, and the situation, there are local decisions being made. Again, I'll use my own specific example from having been in charge of inventory at a chain store.

From 1997 to 1999, I worked as a Product Manager for the Chapters in Ancaster, Ontario. My role was to oversee the inventory for the store. My goal was to maximize margin and inventory turns. But there was also a mandate, with Ancaster being a combination of Hamilton suburb and rural community, to ensure a decent mix of titles that were relevant to the local community.

I was sent merchandising layouts and diagrams and instructions on what books would be placed on what tables and endcaps, what was sanctioned as "co-op" placement. During any given plan, anywhere from 50 to 90% of the prime display areas were spoken for as part of the chain offering their unique brand and consistent flavor.

From the first day the store opened, there were titles and spaces that were controlled by head office; but there were also places that I had control over.

Such as the designated local interest section that was front and center near the main entrance to the store, and where I featured titles about Hamilton, Ancaster, and the surrounding region, but also titles by authors from within a specific geographic radius of the store.

I also reviewed catalogs with sales reps who would come visit me in my store. Some of them were very hands on and would run their own reports, share data on how titles we didn't have in stock might be selling in other regional stores inside and outside the chain, and I would place orders through the store's inventory system. If a title wasn't listed in my store's database, I had the ability to contact the buyer for that merchandising category and request that they add it to my system so I could place an order. I also had the ability to add the title and the publisher manually (in the case of a book acquired from a local publisher that didn't sell to head office buyers), or request that the title be imported back into the company's main head office database.

I also had the ability to special order in books for customers who requested them, or to place orders for in store events.

This is where having an ISBN is critical, because the ISBN is the SKU number that would be used as the primary identifier to track a book in the system. Books without ISBNs could be added in to stock, but that was usually based on manually tracked sheets of paper in a binder, the titles would get rung in and sold under some sort of "dummy" SKU or as a generic sale assigned to a particular category, but then they never showed up as available in the database, and even if it sold hundreds of copies, nobody except the few staff who handled the book would ever even be aware of that title.

Much of this control that I initially had migrated back to head office, which is one of the reasons why I made the change in 1999 from working at the store level and over to head office. And this is also one specific store in Canada. Each chain in each country likely has some sort of similar operation, but they also very likely have their own versions of local control.

And that's where you, as the author, come in.

That's where having a professional relationship with the local bookstore can be helpful.

If you have a new release that is forthcoming and that you are planning, you might consider letting that bookstore you already have a relationship with know about it. The same way they usually know about other forthcoming titles that publishers are releasing in the coming seasons.

Some people consider that people who work in chain retail bookstores are akin to zombies or "pod people" who only follow procedures handed down from the "mother ship" and couldn't care less about the product they are handling. Sure, every single retail shop in the world, particularly chain retail shops, are likely to have their share of those types of people.

But I know, through my own experience working and shopping in chain bookstores, that they are filled with people who are die-hard book lovers. Many of them are avid readers, and they are passionate about reading, about books, and love nothing more than to talk about great books and put the right book into the right customer's hand.

Chain retail booksellers are most likely earning minimum wage. They work hard and are often there out of passion and commitment and love of books.

It is critical to remember that. Just like it is critical to remember that every single person who works in that store is a unique individual with different tastes and aptitudes. One of them might be a potential fan of your work, if given the proper chance.

And, just because you perhaps had a bad experience with a single clerk in a specific store – maybe it was their attitude, the way they treated you or another customer – doesn't mean there's no opportunity of working with them. Perhaps that person was caught at the wrong time on the wrong day and in the wrong mood. Or perhaps there's another staff member there whose passion and desire shines through.

Even if the management of a store isn't receptive to hosting a book signing or stocking your book, there might be a staff member who has you top of mind when dealing with another customer and making a recommendation for a book to read; even if that ends up being a special order.

When I was a bookseller, and I did start off working in a small format chain store, my greatest pleasure was connecting the right reader with the right book. It didn't matter if it was a book currently in stock in my store at the time. If necessary, I would send the customer to the competitor's store down the street or in the mall; I'd suggest they look for it at the library. All I wanted was to help them get that book because I knew they would get value out of the experience.

The focus was on the customer, the reader. Sound familiar? It's not all that different than you, as a writer, putting the reader's consideration front and center in your writing, your overall marketing strategy.

So many of the customers that I sent away in search of that perfect reader/book connection rather than settle for a less ideal book that was in stock, returned to me and the store I worked at, because they knew I wasn't interested in making a sale, I was interested in satisfying their need.

Imagine having a bookseller or two out there who knows about you and your books, and whose passion is about making that same fulfilled customer experience. It shouldn't be hard to imagine, because, in my three decades of bookselling experience, I know there are plenty of other booksellers out there who are like me.

It never hurts to have someone on the inside who is partial to you and your books. That's why getting to know your local bookstore, and spending as much time as possible learning about its specific nuances, the people who work there, the overall unique culture that it has within the larger corporate branding, is so important.

Just remember, when you approach a bookstore, make sure you're already familiar with it, with their traffic patterns, the busy times, the slower times, the time of year. You don't want, for example, to try to get a few minutes of a busy bookseller's time at 4 PM on Christmas Eve, one of the busiest days of the year for a bookseller, to talk about your forthcoming book.

Independent Bookstores

An independent bookstore is a retail bookstore that is independently owned and operated – a small business, a privately owned corporation, partnership, sole proprietorship, or non-profit operation. Independent bookstores usually consist of a single retail location; however, some do operate multiple locations. A few of the larger ones with more than two locations might be considered an independent chain.

While the dawn of online bookselling, the expansion of chains and big box stores, and the emergence of eBooks once threatened independent bookstore operations, causing many to go out of business, they have, in recent years, particularly in the underlying wave of "support local" and "organic" movements in western culture, seen a huge upsurge and growth.

Though it is difficult to fully capture the actual number of independent bookstore operations, the American Booksellers Association boasts over 2,300 member stores. Those are just members. Thousands of other non-member stores exist in communities across the country. The same will hold true in most countries, as so many of those operations, following an independent spirit, may not be members of a central tracking organization.

It would take up too much space to list examples of independent bookstores around the world, however, the resource section at the back of this book provides some places you can find dynamic online lists in some of the larger English language territories.

Before we get into talking about indie bookstores, I thought it would be important to focus on the term "indie" itself and what it means to bookstores and publishers long before self-published authors adopted the term for themselves.

Because, numerous times, I have seen authors from the digital DIY realm, who have adopted "indie author" rather than "self-published" author, be confused and angry about seeing bookstores use that term.

It makes sense to me that authors who take the self-publishing path adopted a term that is more fitting. After all, the only "self" in "self-publishing" is how the entire process is self-directed. The majority of the most successful self-published authors are actually operating small one person or two person businesses. They don't do all the work themselves, they hire out the right professionals, such as editors, cover designers, and others. They are, more aptly, independent publishers.

So, while it is important to use a term more fitting for the actual business an author is in, it's also important to know that, within publishing, that term was already being used. Larger operations which in some cases might be just one or two individuals with traditional Offset printing and warehousing of books, have long been called independent publishers rather than small press publishers. It was a way for them to proudly distinguish themselves from the larger mainstream national multi-national publishers.

In the same way, independently owned, operated, and managed bookstores have proudly shared the fact that they are unique and self-directed and more focused on serving their local community than being part of a cookie-cutter style chain of bookstores.

"Proudly indie" or "fiercely independent" were terms regularly used when describing themselves.

So, if you're an indie author, and you see a bookstore with a sign that says, "Support your local indies!" just remember they are talking about independently run businesses, and not their local indie authors.

However, don't forget that you actually share a very common bond. And that underlying thing you share can be a very good thing.

The ordering, stocking, and returning operations of an independent bookstore is similar, in function, to that of a chain bookstore. The main difference is that the initial frontlist buying decisions and core store offerings aren't made by a remote head office buyer in New York, London, Melbourne, Auckland, or Toronto. They are made right in the store, often by the owner or store manager themselves.

While buying and purchasing decisions can be shared among staff members based on their personal interests, passion, and expertise (rather than a single person having to do the buying for all categories), unlike in chain bookstores, buying typically isn't their sole responsibility. Their buying often occurs as one of many different roles that they play in the store's day to day operations.

This is a wonderful thing, because when you get to know your local booksellers and cultivate a positive relationship with them, you're connecting with the people making those buying decisions. But it can also make it tricky for you when you are looking to get face time with them, as they are often juggling multiple tasks.

I have worked in bookstores where a single bookseller in responsible for stocking shelves, receiving books into stock, running the cash register, answering the phone, reviewing sales reports and re-orders, and assisting customers on the sales floor.

So, if you have ever gotten a "I don't have time for this" look from a bookseller at an independent bookshop, chances are, you caught them in the middle of one of those days.

Always remember the importance of considering the individualist nature of an independent bookstore. They very often represent the culture of the local community and the unique individual personality of the owners, managers, and staff members. Their connection with local customers is often deeply personal and includes a sense of strong loyalty that runs both ways. The customers of an independent bookstore are loyal to that store, more interested in purchasing a book from the bookseller they love than getting that same book at a discounted price in a department store or online. And the booksellers are loyal to their customers, often keeping them in mind with every single book decision they make.

One of the important things you can do is not to ask what your bookstore can do for you, but, instead ask what you can do for your bookstore.

Pacific Northwest Science Fiction author Robert L Slater has cultivated a very special relationship with his hometown Bellingham, Washington independent bookstore Village Books.

Two of Rob's novels, though independently published, are available on the shelves at Village Books as I write this in the fall of 2019. A few of his other titles are available to order from their website or in store. Village Books constantly keeps stock of Rob's books.

They stock the books because the books are professionally produced, satisfy the cravings of their reading audience, and they have a positive and professional relationship with Rob.

Something that the bookstore told Rob when, as a local community author, he was beginning to get to know them, was that he was the first author who approached them and asked him what he could do to help and support them rather than the other way around, which was the basic context of most of their local author interactions prior to that.

Want to stand out as a professional author for a local bookstore? Demonstrate to them that you care enough to learn about them, their needs, the community they serve; and that you're willing to offer something of value that serves those needs.

Another thing to consider, when it comes to independent bookstores, is that the majority of them focus on walk-in traffic and physical book sales. There are some, however, that have an operational website for special orders and also for eBooks and digital audiobooks.

In the US, there are hundreds of independent bookstore locations that are partnered with Rakuten Kobo through the American Booksellers Association for the delivery of eBooks. This allows a customer to set up an account with that bookstore, and to buy and read eBooks either on a Kobo eReader or on a free app for their smartphone or tablet, and the bookstore earns revenue off of that sale. This allows a patron of the bookstore to read eBooks while still supporting their favorite local book shop.

Similarly, Hummingbird Digital Media delivers digital audiobooks and eBooks to independent bookstores via a platform called MyMustReads.com. There is a partnership with the American Booksellers Association, but according to their website, the company is also open to working with bookstores anywhere.

Libro.fm digital audiobooks offer a similar system where a patron can tie their account to their favorite local bookstore and purchase audiobooks while knowing that they are still tied to and supporting their local bookstore. You can find a listing of independent bookstores that participate in one or more of these programs via Indiebound.org.

And, if your local bookstore is participating, why not include a link to your bookstore on that bookstore's website rather than just to Amazon and the online retailers?

If you are appearing at a book signing at that store, and a potential reader indicates they read eBooks, you can help the bookstore by letting the customer know they can get the book via the bookstore's website. You might even go one step further by appearing with postcards that you can create via VistaPrint with the book cover on it, but a link to the eBook or audiobook on the book's website (a written out link plus an easily scannable QR code so they can quickly access it on their smartphone). But whatever you do, don't show up at an independent bookstore with handouts that drive them to buy the eBook at a competitor.

Academic Bookstores

Academic bookstores are stores concerned with supplying reading material for an adjacent college, university or vocational institution. The books they stock might be for students, in the way of required reading and other course-specific materials, but might also include general trade titles for the non-academic reading of that institution's staff members. Although often, the trade titles are likely to skew more toward the academic community.

In one way, an academic bookstore might be considered a type of niche market, which I will explore below.

For example, when I worked at the bookstore at McMaster University in Hamilton, Ontario, it not only sold textbooks and other course materials, but it carried more than 40,000 general trade books. This was about 30,000 more titles than the average local mall store, and 60,000 less than the nearest Chapters big box store location. It also contained a much broader, or deeper selection of titles associated with academic disciplines. If you walked into Chapters, for example, you might find trade books with a focus on engineering mixed into a general science section. But at McMaster's bookstore, there would be multiple shelves of engineering-oriented books, many exploring, in-depth, the various types of engineering disciplines.

Some academic bookstores are owned and operated by the university. Many of them consider themselves independent. Queens University Bookstore in Kingston, Ontario, for example, is owned and directed by the student society. And, when I was at McMaster, the bookstore was overseen by the Department of Student Affairs, with all profits benefiting student services on campus. Many stores, like in these two examples, are independently operated and their business procedures, when it comes to trade or general interest books, are similar to the spirit of independent booksellers. The same, of course, is true for completely independent bookstores that operate off campus. I remember, for example, when attending Carleton University in Ottawa, Ontario, that many of my English professors sent us to Octopus Books, a community-based co-op bookstore in the city, rather than to the on campus bookstore.

Other academic bookstores are part of a large corporate chain. Follett is one of the companies that operates these stores, much in the same manner that large big box chain retailers operate.

A significant difference in the way that academic bookstores operate, particularly when it comes to the required readings, is that the textbook and course material buyers don't meet with publishing sales reps. Instead, the sales reps visit the faculty members, each trying to convince the faculty that their textbook and supporting course materials are better than the other brand's version of the same. The instructor then lets the textbook buyers know what titles they want as required and optional reading, and the buyers source those.

This process if often called "textbook adoption." When a faculty member adopts a textbook for a course, it means that they are going to be informing their students to read that particular book, and the bookstore, which has access to knowing how many students are in the class, orders in enough copies to fulfill the expected need.

If your book is appropriate for a particular discipline and you are able to get the attention of a college or university instructor, having your book adopted as a required textbook can be akin to a winning lottery ticket. This is because having a single "fan" as a college instructor, can lead to hundreds of sales each new semester.

Academic bookstores also normally receive what is called a "short discount" from academic publishers for their books. This is typically 20%. While you will hear every seemingly logical explanation for this in the world from insiders, it comes down to this. The academic publisher knows that the bookstore has no choice but to order whatever book the faculty member requests; therefore, there's no incentive for them to offer a more appealing discount. It's not as if the bookstore has a choice or can buy it anywhere else, except maybe through the used book channels and student buyback programs. Traditional publishers have long leveraged this "monopoly" strategy and upheld a pricing and discount model that is inverse from every single other retail setting, including general interest trade books.

One reason that I note this is that if your book is something being considered by a faculty member, and it is available to the bookstore for a 40% discount or more, that makes the book even more appealing; particularly in the case of an academic bookstore where the profit goes back to supporting student services.

Don't forget, however, that the same conditions for ordering and stocking books exists as you will find within general trade brick and mortar bookstores. Returns. So an order of 500 copies of a book doesn't mean a permanent sale. Unsold copies can be returned at the end of the term, and those returns often cost more than what was earned in the sale.

Niche, Genre, and Specialty Bookstores

Within both chain and independent operations, you will find speciality bookstores. These are shops that have chosen a particular niche. Their goal is to focus on that niche and to serve them exclusively.

These niche markets might be small, or they might be huge. But these stores are not attempting to appeal to everyone; just the core group of readers.

Some examples of these types of speciality shops are Children's, Christian, Used, and genre-specific like Mystery, Romance, or Science-Fiction and Fantasy.

Eso Won Books, in Los Angeles, California, which specializes in African American books is going to pay attention to different things for their customer base than Bakka-Phoenix, a Science-Fiction and Fantasy store in Toronto, Ontario. Just like Woozles, a children's bookstore in Halifax, Nova Scotia is likely to concern themselves differently than Treadwell's Bookshop, in London, UK, that specializes in books for the practicing occultist and wizard.

Depending on how your book and any specific connection might play into those niche markets, this can be something that works out exceptionally in your favor, or, on the other hand, inform you it would be a waste of time for both you and the bookstore to pursue.

Important Things to Remember about Brick-and-Mortar Bookstores

In the same way that social media is expressed as an interactive community rather than as a "sales" tool with 80% of your activity being about engaging and giving to the community and 20% of it being about asking or selling, the same thing holds true.

An author who is a part of the community stands a better chance of cultivating a real relationship with their local bookseller and being able to find the right connection for the right book, to make the acquisition possible.

It is only through speaking with and getting to know the different people in the store that you might happen upon someone who loves to read the type of book that you write or shares your passion for reading. There is a natural bridge there, where, when they discover this, they rejoice in the thrill of hand-selling your book to the right customer.

Some of my favorite, most memorable experiences as a bookseller involve the magic that happens when the right customer at the right time is looking for the right book, and it happens to be a book from a local author, or an author who I recently interacted with in my store, at a remote event, or even online.

But outside of genre or reading taste, remember, one element that is usually important are the local author factor. Does the store have a local interest or local author section? Let them know, when the timing is right, about your book. Or maybe, even if you are not local to the store itself, there is something about your book's setting or the origin of the characters that relate to that store's locale.

Look at the local store's layout to see if there is any sort of event space. Check the store's printed in store handout or online or email newsletter. Do they have events? What sorts of events do they hold? Readings, book signings, talks, lectures, workshops? Is there something from your experience either as a writer, or in the research of your writing, or in the books you have, that can help fulfill this type of event?

Those are the things that are easiest to pitch to a bookstore.

It's not about you or about your book – it's about the unique experience that you and the presence of your book can mean, which can, in turn, result in sales for the bookstore.

Basically, what can you offer to the store to help them attract more traffic and sell more books?

Techniques and Ideas for Approaching Bookstores

Now that we have taken a look at the different bookstores, and the different ways that decisions are made, let's look at some ideas and techniques that might work.

Bear in mind that these ideas are being outlined in a generic fashion, or, in some cases, delve into specific examples. It is critical that you read these with the idea of applying all the unique elements associated with you, your book, and the bookstore in question before you develop a specific plan that caters to that situation.

First, make sure that you fully understand your book, who the ideal audience is, what need the book fulfills and how it serves the reading community. Consider how your book matches or offers some sort of cross-over with the consumers that are likely to be customers of that bookstore. Which means that, prior to contact, you'll have had to have done some deep thinking and research. Don't forget that it might not just be the book, but it could be you, and your author brand, or something about the research you put into the book that might provide the value for that bookstore and its customers.

If there is an event related to your book and the bookstore offers events, consider the proposed format of such an event (reading, talk, workshop, etc) and whether or not you've done something successful like that in the past. If you have, perhaps even including a contact for a reference from another store, or even a library, where you held a successful event can help.

Create a pitch based on these things. Practice that pitch. Practice it verbally. Practice writing it down.

Be prepared to drop off or mail a print copy of your book to the bookstore with a one-page cover letter that talks about it, including elements related to how it fulfills a need that is pertinent to that bookstore. It is critical that this letter includes details about where and how the book is available for the bookstore to purchase.

Within traditional publishing, most publishers produce ARCs (Advance Reader Copies) of books to be sent to bookstore buyers or reviewers. If you are traditionally published, make sure your publisher or the publicist you are in contact with has the address of the bookstore and the name, if you know it, of the right person(s) to send that copy to.

If you are independently published, the onus falls on you to create additional promotionally copies like this. Consider this. For every 100 authors independently publishing a book like yours, how many of them have taken the time to print off a promotional copy to provide a local bookstore? You might have to pay to play for that book, listed among millions of other titles on Amazon, to stand out. So, consider the cost of a printed book in order to stand out in a more professional and dynamic way.

If you already have a relationship with the bookstore, contacting them or providing an ARC or proof copy of the book should be easy.

Just be prepared for the fact that you are giving this book away and may never get a sale from it via the bookstore. But there are side effects, in terms of your impression to that store and the booksellers, as a professional, and there might be other side-effects too.

For example, having been a bookseller, I've received thousands of ARC copies of books over the years. Most of them I have never taken home – many more I have never read. Some of them I've passed along to other booksellers, or even loyal regular bookstore customers, because it was a book I felt they would love. Sometimes I put the book on a shelf to read at a later date. One, I remember picking up and reading 10 years after receiving it. No, the publisher and the author didn't get anything from me when I first received it. But after reading that 10-year old ARC, I went out and bought every single book in print by that author. Then, I ordered that author's books into stock at my bookstore and continued to hand-sell those books to the right readers.

That's long-term thinking. It's a dramatically different approach than looking at your *Kindle Direct Publishing* dashboard every fifteen minutes to see if you've gotten another sale.

If you don't have a relationship with the bookstore, it's likely best to email or call the store. If you call, be sure to ask if it is a good time to speak with them, and who you should speak with to let them know about your book. It might be the owner, a consignment manager, or an events coordinator that you are directed to.

The business might be completed via a call, or it might be the opportunity to book an in-person meeting. Be prepared to be flexible for the store's needs, and make sure you have that pre-practiced pitch information handy, as well as a calendar, on the chance that, should you be pitching an event to the bookstore, they want to look at potential dates.

Keep the following details in mind and handy, because these are likely the things the bookstore is curious about knowing.

- What is the book about and how does this book help fit the needs of the bookstore and its customers?
- What special expertise makes you the ideal person to deliver this book or this event to that store's customers?
- How is the book available for the bookstore to order, and under what terms of sale? And under what terms of returnability?
- Where and how can the bookstore find out more information about you, your books, and how to order them?

For in person, email and phone conversations, it can be extremely useful to have prepared a single page sell-sheet. This is an attractive flyer-like one-page document that includes your book cover image and details about the book; this would be similar in the way that a book might be presented in a publisher's print catalog.

In the online resources that accompany this book, you will find a few examples of one-page sell-sheets as examples of the types of things that might capture a bookseller's interest.

Book Event Etiquette

It is important to demonstrate professionalism and engagement at all three stages of any event that you manage to secure with a bookstore.

Prior. Promotion is important. Advertise and share via social media, your author newsletter, and on your website. Don't just rely on the store to draw a crowd. Make sure you leverage your own contacts and outreach so that it's a team effort.

During. Be conscious of how you treat staff, behave and interact with customers, even those who aren't interested in your book. People will remember how you made them feel. And tips on having a display about ten feet away (for safety and introverts).

After. Acknowledgement and thanks are important. Take the time to send the bookstore a note thanking them for being gracious hosts. Extend kudos and thanks to any staff that went out of their way to be helpful or offer a positive experience either to you or something you witnesses them doing when engaging with a customer.

TIPS FOR WHEN YOUR BOOK IS POD AND/OR NON-RETURNABLE

As we discussed earlier, while print on demand titles are fantastic for online listings, and just in time one-off copy inventory shipments, they can sometimes be prohibitive to bookstores being willing to order and stock the titles on their shelves.

There might come a time when you have a great opportunity to do a book-related event at your local bookstore, and it is something that can be beneficial for you, your author brand, and the bookstore, but your book is non-returnable. This can be from a combination of factors:

1) That's the way your publisher set it up (as a POD/non-returnable title)
2) That's the way you set it up yourself as an independent publisher (either via *IngramSpark*, or some other POD service provider)
3) The publisher/distributor of your book is too far away geographically that returns are a cost-prohibitive behavior for the bookstore

You might, at first, believe that you are in a no-win situation. However, there might be some creative solutions that can act to potentially turn it into a positive experience.

It is something that might work should you have a decent, open, and honest relationship with the bookstore;

and if they are willing to consider flexible alternatives to the way that they normally run their business.

Sometimes, if the business case works out, and the bookstore recognizes a solid commercial viability for placing such an order and stocking a title that is non-returnable, it works itself out.

But what if the commercial viability is nowhere near being a sure thing? Or if it makes the bookstore nervous?

Ask them if they would consider ordering in a specific quantity of the book if they could be guaranteed to sell all copies and not be burdened with a pile of what they might consider "dead stock" that they might be stuck with and have to eventually write-off.

Most bookstores have a staff-discount policy.

In the majority of the situations that I have experienced in more than three decades of bookselling, the staff discount is usually in the realm of 30% off the retail price.

This is a typical default discount because the standard discount that a bookstore receives from a publisher or book distributor is in the realm of 40% to 50%.

Staff discounts, of 30%, usually leave the store with a 10% margin, which is necessary to help them cover their costs. (Remember, they have to pay rent, utilities, staff costs, shipping and receiving costs, software costs, and more). If the discount from the publisher is higher, then the store has a slightly higher margin to play with.

Ten percent might seem like a lot, but even with a full 50% margin on books, that's still such a small sliver of margin, and one of the smallest margins in the retail market. Non-book items, such as clothing and giftware usually have a margin of anywhere between fifty percent at the far low end, to several hundred percent at the high end.

I'm highlighting that difference so that you understand the potential reluctance you might face from a bookstore, that most likely can't operate a successful business on only a 10% margin.

Their operating costs are likely far too high for 10% to cover it.

However, this is merely for a relatively small quantity – let's say 50 books at the most and in a limited fashion.

It is certainly cheaper than having to write-off 100% of the book's value in the case of something that is no longer sellable.

And, when you actually do the math, even if the book IS fully returnable, it would likely cost the bookstore more in labor, supplies, and shipping to have to package up and return a book.

You might consider making an offer to buy up any remaining stock that is left over at the end of the event. This helps reduce the risk that the bookstore is taking. Because, if your event is a huge success, and they sell a ton of copies, they are happy. But, even if nobody shows up and they don't sell a single book, they can still not be stuck with additional "dead" stock, and they, at least, moved some units through the store.

An additional side-effect, of course, might be if the store is one of those reporting sales to local media (for local bestseller lists), or to a state, province, or federal tracking program for bestselling titles.

WORKING WITH LIBRARIES

The Magic of Libraries

I STILL FONDLY remember one of my very first visits to the local public library when I was a child. I lived in a small town of less than two thousand people in Mid-Northern Ontario. The nearest bookstore was about an hour away, but my small hometown of Levack had a public library.

And the public library was a truly magical place.

My mom and I could go there, select a stack of books I wanted to read, and we could bring them home. Then the next week we would return those titles and we'd get a whole new pile of new books. It was a truly wondrous and marvelous experience for me. I imagine your own interactions with your local library when you were growing up might have been a similar, wonderful experience.

I am making that assumption, because I'm assuming that you are a writer. And obviously, something got you into writing. Chances are very likely that it was reading; perhaps it was reading at an early age. And I'm willing to speculate that the library was somehow involved.

I so appreciated my earliest experiences with the library that I made sure to continue that personal childhood tradition of weekly library visits with my son when he was quite young.

Every Saturday morning, we would get up and head to the neighborhood library where we'd negotiate the selection of a stack of books to take home that I could read to him throughout the week.

He would also select books that he planned on either reading, or leafing through on his own. As he got older, I proudly remember that moment when he got his very own library card. To me, it was like passing him the power of Thor's hammer or the majesty of Excalibur, or perhaps more accurately showing him the doorway to countless worlds and experiences.

That's what a library is. It isn't just a building filled with books. It's a dynamic part of energy that opens up the world to quench thirsty minds.

As an author, you currently have three main formats of books that you can get into the library: Print, ebook, and audiobook.

I'll likely have to update this into a new edition should technology create a new format that we haven't yet thought of. (Don't laugh; I still have print books on the bookshelves in my home that never seemed to even imagine the possibilities that would come with digital publishing).

So, if you are reading this far into the future and well beyond 2019, chances are there are newer and exciting formats for books. The reason I say that is because we're still at the early days of the digital revolution of publishing and storytelling.

But I digress.

Let's get back to those three formats of print, eBook and audiobook; and let's break our approach down to the three simple things that you need in order to work with and get you and your books into libraries.

The Three A's of Library Strategy

I like to approach working with libraries by breaking it down into three main elements you need to understand and create a strategy for.

First, you must ensure your book is available to libraries. Second, you need to ensure that the library is aware of your book. And third, the library has to have the desire to acquire your book.

I call this *The Three A's of Library Strategy*.

The three A's are *Availability*, *Awareness*, and *Acquisition*. If you haven't already noticed, I have a thing for alliteration. What can I say? Alliteration is a technique that helps me to remember strategies, processes and logistical approaches. Perhaps you'll also find it handy.

Availability

Availability: Print Books

I'm starting with print because it is perhaps the most common format that we think about when we turn our attention to libraries.

First, let's look at how this works if you are traditionally published.

By traditionally published, I mean that you have sold or licensed your book to a publisher; typically, a publisher that does Offset printing rather than POD or print on demand printing.

This isn't to say that publishers whose main operation involves POD aren't properly traditional publishers, but that line has blurred significantly with the advent of digital publishing, and, as we explored earlier in the book and in the chapter on bookstores, it is important to distinguish the difference between POD distribution and warehoused distribution using Offset printing.

And that's what I'm talking about when I say "traditionally published."

If you are traditionally published, then that publisher likely has warehousing and has direct library sales channels or is already set up to sell their books through Ingram or Baker and Taylor, which are two of the English language, world's largest wholesalers of print books.

This means that can likely skip ahead to the *Awareness* segment, since the availability is mostly handled for you.

If you are traditionally published with a smaller publishing house that uses POD or print on demand printing, then those books might still be available to libraries, most likely via Ingram. It is important to understand this aspect of the publisher you are working with. And I would advise if you have signed the rights to a book to any publisher that you double check and ask your publisher where and how libraries can purchase their books.

I know, for example, that the books I've published through Dundurn, a Toronto based publisher, are printed and stored in a warehouse and made available to libraries and bookstores through UTP distribution in Canada, and that they're also available in the US through Ingram.

My self-published books are not printed through a traditional publishing house nor printed in large volume Offset printing to be stored in warehouses; they are print on demand or POD titles. They are supplied to bookstores and libraries when an order is placed or when demand is created. I know they are available to the libraries and they're available via Ingram's print on demand service.

If you are looking at POD, which is the most barrier free entrance into self-publishing in print, the best, most direct way for you to get into Ingram's system is using *IngramSpark*.

IngramSpark is an author friendly front end to get your book into Ingram's print on demand catalog. You can also get the book into Ingram's catalog via other sources. Some service providers do offer library distribution as well. I know, for example, that *Draft2Digital* print, which is currently in beta at the time of this writing, goes through IPG, which is a distribution company that represents a lot of independent publishers in the United States to warehouse and distribute their books. They also send the digital print book files via Ingram, POD distribution network for global POD availability.

So, if you're using some other POD service for your self-published book, check with them to see how their books are made available to libraries.

A Note of Caution: Many authors use Amazon *KDP Print*, which is free, and is a great way to get your book in Amazon's catalog. It is probably the best way to get your POD book in Amazon's catalog. But do be aware that their *extended distribution* option isn't as attractive nor as appealing to libraries. This is likely due to the crappy terms that are offered to bookstores and libraries; non-returnable and short discounts. These terms are much worse than the library would most likely get if you set up the distribution for it via *IngramSpark*.

In addition, some libraries might actually be opposed to the idea that they're ordering books from Amazon. That could actually be something that puts them off. I know it definitely puts off bookstores, particularly independent bookstores that are feeling the competition from Amazon.

It's like saying: "Hey, bookstore, go and order my book from the big giant monolithic company that's trying to put you out of business. Go and order it from your worst competitor." That is not always something that is going to be received in a positive fashion.

As mentioned in the chapter on bookstores, I actually often jokingly refer to Amazon's *extended distribution* option for POD titles as "pretended distribution" – because it gives you the impression that you're actually reaching a global print market. You are partially reaching it; but with terms that might not be good for anyone on the receiving end; good only for Amazon.

So, you can certainly use Amazon extended distribution, but just be aware that you might get some pushback from libraries, which might negatively impact both the awareness and the acquisition.

It is a case where availability may be there, but awareness and acquisition might be reduced in some cases. And in that same vein, if you are using *IngramSpark* to make your POD book available to libraries, the authors that I know with the most success selling into those channels have usually selected the deepest discount available, which is 55%.

I know that it means a deeper hit on your margin, and sometimes it requires having to lift your retail price a little more to compensate for that. But that larger discount can be appealing to the buyers at libraries. And while bookstores are also looking for non-returnable terms, the library purchasing model isn't about returns.

You do stand a much better chance of library acquisition than you do bookstore acquisition. And that's a great thing to consider when you think about the reach that libraries have into different communities.

Now that we have taken a look at print books, let's move on to availability of eBooks.

Availability: eBooks

Similar to what I mentioned in relation to print books, if you are traditionally published, check with your publisher to ensure they are distributing your eBook to the library market, and see if you can confirm which library wholesalers they are using. At the very least, they should have access to at least OverDrive and Baker & Taylor, two of the larger library distributors.

And, if your publisher is in that continually growing grey zone of calling themselves a "traditional publisher" without having actual legacy publishing warehouse distribution (ie, if they are a born-digital and digital-only publisher), do confirm that they are making the eBook available to libraries.

Cautionary Note: If their terms are author-friendly, there is nothing wrong with a digital-first, or digital-only publisher, particularly one that focuses on eBooks. But do be aware that some outfits that sell themselves as "traditional publishers" and use a digital-only approach to publishing might be locking your book into exclusivity with Amazon *KDP Select*. This makes the book available to Amazon customers to read in Kindle Unlimited (also referred to by many indie authors as "KU"). But it also limits the book from being available at any other retailer or through any library. It is, for each 90-day period of *KDP Select* enrollment, exclusive to Amazon.

So, if you are trusting either a publisher or a publishing services provider, just double check to make sure they are making the eBook available to the library platforms or library wholesalers.

If you are self-publishing your eBook and are in full control of the distribution, there are a number of library wholesale distributors that exist and can help you get your books into the library markets.

I'm not going to outline any sort of authoritative list of these platforms, because this is likely to continue to evolve and change, but at the time of this writing, you can use places such as *Smashwords*, *Draft2Digital*, *StreetLib*, *PublishDrive*, and *Kobo Writing Life*, to get your eBook into the various channels that serve the library markets.

There are other options such as *SELF-e*, which is a joint venture from Library Journal and Biblioboard. It's designed to expose self-published eBooks to more readers via public libraries. Distribution through *SELF-e* though, is royalty free, which means authors don't earn royalties, do not get compensated through this platform. *SELF-e* might best be seen as a marketing tool to build a readership through library channels. But for the purposes of this segment, I would much rather focus on the opportunities that allow you both exposure and income in the library market.

Call that a little biased nuance of mine; preferring that authors are compensated for their work with money.

As the expression goes, particularly when someone is trying to over-sell me on something by saying that the exposure will be good for me as an author, I often tell them that a person can die from exposure.

OverDrive is the world's leading digital reading platform for libraries and schools, delivering the book industry's largest catalog of eBooks, audiobooks and other digital media to more than 43,000 libraries in 75 countries. For English language books, there is no doubt that they should be included in your strategy for getting your digital books into libraries.

So, let's spend a little bit of time focusing on them. First of all, it is possible to have a direct account with OverDrive.

It is possible, but difficult.

And it is something I would not advise.

Based on my personal experience and from speaking with dozens of bigger name indie authors who were able to establish a direct account with OverDrive over the years, it's likely not worth your time, hassle and struggle to try to establish a direct account. Simply, the systems and the methods to get titles into their systems directly are painful and extremely manual and require understanding and using FTP and Excel files and a whole world of frustration that'll remind you (if, like me, you're of a certain age) of the "Press play on tape one" days of computing.

In all seriousness, the people at OverDrive are among the nicest and most passionate book nerds you will ever meet. They are amazing; wonderful to work with (I've had the pleasure of knowing many of them for years), and they have a long-established wonderful relationship with libraries. But their systems are not optimized for small publishers or indie authors communicating directly with their business. Their systems are optimized to serve the library community, which is their forte and why you want to be in their catalog.

So, from a completely business-minded point of view, there's no need for OverDrive to waste time and resources building out an author friendly front end, because they have no shortage of third-party companies and even sister companies that specialize in getting titles into their system.

Speaking of sister companies, let's start with Kobo and *Kobo Writing Life*.

Kobo and OverDrive are sister companies both owned by Rakuten, Inc. You may notice that the official names for the companies are actually *Rakuten Kobo Inc.* and *Rakuten OverDrive*. Rakuten is a major Japanese ecommerce and online retail company that originated in Tokyo. It is often referred to as the "Amazon of Japan."

Because of the fact that Kobo and OverDrive are subsidiary companies, and also because of the months I spent negotiating with colleagues at OverDrive when I was running *Kobo Writing Life* (the direct-to-Kobo self publishing platform), if you make your books available to OverDrive via *Kobo Writing Life*, you get the same margin that you do if you had an account directly with OverDrive.

You get all the benefit of the full direct margin without any of the hassle of the tech stuff that you have to deal with when working direct with OverDrive. That margin is 50% of the library list price.

This means, if you set a library price of $10 you would make $5 every time a library buys a single copy of one of your eBooks. This is done under what's known as either a one-to-one or a *one copy, one user* licensing model.

This means that if a library system, New York Public Library, for example, buys a copy of your eBook, they can loan it to one NYPL patron at a time, forever. You get paid a decent amount upfront for the book, 50% but only ever see that money once, because the library now has a permanent copy they can continue to re-loan.

And, unlike a print book, where wear and tear might lead to them purchasing another copy (if a book were so popular that it would warrant that), there is no wear and tear on an eBook.

This *one copy, one user* model via *Kobo Writing Life*, which offers you 50% is the highest margin that you'll make from any third-party provider to overdrive.

If you use *Smashwords*, that same *one copy, one user* model gets you 45%. If you use *Draft2Digital*, you get about 47%.

However, with *Draft2Digital*, there is an additional model that isn't currently available via *Kobo Writing Life*. If you make your book available to OverDrive via *Draft2Digital*, there's also an option to opt into the CPC or *cost per checkout* model.

The *cost per checkout* model for libraries is a different type of system. In this model, a library is able to get access to the same title for more than one user at a time, and instead of a fixed higher margin of 45%, 47%, or 50% of the library list price, they actually pay one tenth of the eBook's full list price each time the book is loaned out.

Here's how that difference works.

For a book that I have listed with the US dollar retail price of $4.99 I may have the library list price at $6.99. That would mean that via *Kobo Writing Life*, I'd have the single option of *one copy, one user*, and I would make $3.49 cents per sale to a library market. In that same model, I would make $3.27 via *Draft2Digital*.

In this case, *KWL* nets 22 cents more than *D2D*.

But in a *cost per checkout* model, which *Kobo Writing Life* doesn't currently have, I'd make 46 cents every time a patron checks that book out.

I would make less up front than I would in that *one copy one user* model, but after more than seven people have checked out the eBook, I would start to earn more than I would for that single sale.

In my own experience, particularly with the *cost per checkout* model from audiobooks, those residual smaller payments can really add up.

Imagine that your book is being read by a local book club. Some people are going to buy the print book and some are going to buy the eBook. Some are going to flock to their local library for either the print or eBook editions.

If the book club is a library specific book club, then there'd be a higher demand for one particular branch of the library to have more than one copy of the book. So, either the library has to spend their budget on buying multiple copies, or only one lucky reader will have access to it at a time, while the others are on a waiting list and can only read that copy when they finish.

That's not ideal for a book club, where all the members want to be reading simultaneously.

However, in the *cost per checkout* model, an unlimited number of people could check out the book at the exact same time. Let's imagine that there were 20 people in this library branch book club. They could all check out the book all at the exact same time and quickly earn you far more than the single copy sold to a library.

Remember that *cost per checkout* does come with a short-term reduction of margin, but also with ongoing earning benefits of smaller payments that might, in the long run work out to be worth more.

For my own personal strategy, I am more leaning towards that long-term CPC or *cost per checkout* option. As I've mentioned, I've already seen some decent success in that realm already within audiobooks.

There are plenty of other library distribution options available. Baker and Taylor, Bibliotheca, and hoopla are among the other options that libraries regularly use.

Draft2Digital can, for example, get your eBook into those markets and more. Each of these library wholesalers uses either a *one copy per user* or *cost per checkout* model. Some library channels, like OverDrive, utilize a combination of both.

Recommended eBook Pricing Strategy

Platforms like *Kobo Writing Life*, *Smashwords* and *Draft2Digital* allow you to set and control your library price separate from your retail price.

KWL and *Draft2Digital* typically advise that authors set their library price at anywhere between 1.5 to 3 times their regular retail price.

The reason for this is because of the previously mentioned *one copy, one user* licensing model for library sales. In this model, when a library purchases your eBook, they can loan that single copy of the eBook to one customer at a time, forever. This means that, unlike in regular retail channel sales, where you earn money every time a new customer buys your book, you only get paid once via a library sale. That library sale, then, is valued higher.

This strategic pricing strategy also keeps in mind the stark realty that most of the major publishers, whose retail price for eBooks is typically two to three times the retail price for independently published titles, similarly set significantly higher library prices. The average retail list price of a new release from a big publisher can range from $9.99 to $19.99 USD. When it comes to library list prices, those same titles might be priced anywhere between $30 to $80 USD.

While independent author eBook retail prices for full length books have slowly walked up over the years from the realm of $0.99, $1.99, and $2.99 USD, the majority of retail sales typically happens in the $3.99 to $8.99 USD realm for most of those successful authors.

This pricing strategy is used partially as an obvious value offer for readers, but also as a way to remove the barrier from a reader who might be interested in checking out a writer whose work they are not familiar with.

Personally, while I respect a strategy that makes eBooks more affordable for readers, I still think that self-published authors default to under-valuing their work in the same way that traditional publishers outrageously over-price their books. But let's not get me started on that lengthy and heated discussion, except to say that I believe indie authors can still offer competitive prices on their eBooks without having to practically give them away. A well written, well-edited, and professionally produced book is all a reader wants. And most readers are willing to pay a fair and reasonable price for their six to eight hours of reading pleasure.

In keeping with this type of competitive pricing strategy for the library market, you'd be advised to consider that 1.5 to 3 times your retail price when pricing for the library market.

For example, here are some potential price models based on the low (1.5X) to the higher end (3X).

$2.99 USD Retail Price
- $4.99 USD Library Price (Retail X 1.5, rounded up)
- $5.99 USD Library Price (Retail X 2, rounded up)
- $8.99 USD Library Price (Retail X 3, rounded up)

$3.99 USD Retail Price
- $5.99 USD Library Price (Retail X 1.5, rounded up)
- $7.99 USD Library Price (Retail X 2, rounded up)
- $11.99 USD Library Price (Retail X 3, rounded up)

$4.99 USD Retail Price
- $7.99 USD Library Price (Retail X 1.5, rounded up)
- $9.99 USD Library Price (Retail X 2, rounded up)
- $14.99 USD Library Price (Retail X 3, rounded up)

$5.99 USD Retail Price
- $8.99 USD Library Price (Retail X 1.5, rounded up)
- $11.99 USD Library Price (Retail X 2, rounded up)
- $17.99 USD Library Price (Retail X 3, rounded up)

$6.99 USD Retail Price
- $10.99 USD Library Price (Retail X 1.5, rounded up)
- $13.99 USD Library Price (Retail X 2, rounded up)
- $20.99 USD Library Price (Retail X 3, rounded up)

$7.99 USD Retail Price
- $11.99 USD Library Price (Retail X 1.5, rounded up)
- $15.99 USD Library Price (Retail X 2, rounded up)
- $23.99 USD Library Price (Retail X 3, rounded up)

I only illustrated examples between $2.99 to $7.99 USD in the examples above because the majority of indie authors who are selling in high volume in 2019 are typically using retail pricing in that range.

You'll also notice that, in the lower realm of the pricing, the 3X pricing is still quite competitive and low. But, as you get to the higher price points, the 3X pricing option begins to look more like the over-priced traditionally published books. While I might personally default to using two or three times my retail price for my lower priced eBooks, when I look at my books that are priced a bit higher, I tend to adjust that calculation default to one point five or two times.

You should be aware that librarians will often look to see what your regular retail price is on the major eBook platforms. Because, while your library price is most likely significantly more affordable than the pricing of comparable titles from the major publishers, they also don't want to feel like you are ripping them off.

For example, if your regular retail price for a novel is $0.99 USD and your library price is $9.99 USD your pricing model is ten times higher for libraries and might be construed as a greedy move.

If, as a "classically trained" indie author who is most comfortable with significantly lower pricing on your books, setting a library price that is any sort of multiplication higher than the retail price makes you squirm and fidget in your seat, consider this: in the *one copy, one user* library licensing model, you will typically only ever sell a single copy to any library system. This means that library permanently owns that copy and can loan it out, to one patron at a time, forever, and you only ever earn that money once.

Let's say that over the course of a year 1000 people are interested in reading your latest book.

Let's also assume (just to keep things simple) that 500 of those people buy your book on Amazon and the other 500 rush to get it from their local library.

And let's also assume that, because you are thoughtful and generous, (on top of being incredibly talented as a storyteller – I mean, *that* should go without saying) you set a retail price of $0.99 USD and set the library price at $1.99 USD.

For each single copy library sale, you likely earned between $0.89 and $1.00. Let's pretend, then, that you sell 5 copies, one to a number of major urban library centers across the US. This means that your library earnings, for 500 people to read your book, work out to between $4.45 and $5.00 USD.

But, even earning only 35% royalties (which you get on a book priced at $0.99 USD on Amazon), you'd collect $175 USD for those 500 new readers.

Those pennies, over time, can really add up. Or not add up, as the case might be, in the long run.

Availability: Audiobooks

In the same way that Amazon is a household name and most authors who are looking at publishing eBooks are familiar with Kindle and *KDP*, they are also familiar with the digital audiobook service Audible (which is owned by Amazon) and *ACX* (*Audiobook Creation*

Exchange), the gateway for authors to get their work in to Audible, Amazon, and iTunes (which recently rebranded as Apple Books).

While *ACX* does offer a royalty share option that requires absolutely no cash up front (opting to share their earned margin with a narrator), making it easier for authors to break into the audio market, that option comes with a cost of 7 years of exclusivity.

Similarly, even if you pay up front for the narrator's work, *ACX* has a parallel 7-year exclusivity clause that earns authors a higher royalty rate from Audible.

If your audiobook is locked into exclusivity with ACX, then it will not be available into the library market.

There is a way out of exclusivity, if you are looking for one. As of November 2019, the following is true: If the audiobook was completed as a *Pay-for-Production* deal, (meaning you paid for the narrator's work up front), the distribution rights can be changed from exclusive to non-exclusive after it has been on sale in stores for one year. If, however, your audiobook is in a *Royalty Share* deal, the agreement cannot be changed.

If you are interested in getting your audiobook in to the library systems, your two main choices include *Author's Republic* and *Findaway Voices*.

Both of those companies have broad distribution options that include library markets such as OverDrive, Baker & Taylor, Bibliotheca, hoopla, and Odilo.

In my particular case, and the platform that I'm most familiar with for getting audiobooks into the library market is using *Findaway Voices*. So, I will specifically talk about their process; but be aware that *Author's Republic* does offer a similar service.

With *Findaway Voices*, you can get your audiobook into the following library markets: Overdrive, Baker & Taylor, Bibliotheca, hoopla, Odilo, Bidi, Ebscoe, Follett, MLOL, 3Leaf Group, Perma-Bound and Wheelers. These library systems all have either a la carte, which works like the *one copy one user* model discussed for eBooks, or a *cost per checkout* model. In some of the library markets, such as OverDrive, Bibliotheca and Odilo, both are available. And, like eBooks, you have the ability of creating a unique library price as opposed to the regular retail price. This means that you can set special prices just for the library market.

Findaway Voices is part of a larger audiobook distribution company called Findaway. Findaway might be considered as the Ingram for the digital audiobook market. Among other things, Findaway boasts the world's largest catalog available for the retail and library market, with close to a quarter of a million titles from more than 2400 international publishers.

When you make your audiobook available through *Findaway Voices*, you can leverage this distribution platform, and always have the choice to which specific downstream networks you wish to distribute to via a per-title opt-in process.

Recommended Audiobook Pricing Strategy

Findaway Voices allows you to set and control a separate and distinct library price for your audiobook. They have a built-in tool based on details from sales volumes, per genre that can suggest an optimal price for your audiobook.

The pricing strategy algorithm they use is complex and dynamic and is not something that can be replicated here. But it does result in showing you three suggested price range options for your audiobook: Minimum Recommended; Findaway Recommended; Maximum Recommended.

Awareness and Acquisition

I'm going to cover awareness and acquisition in a joint fashion because the two coexist and play well off of one another.

Just having your book listed as available to the library systems does not necessarily mean that libraries will even see or order your book. So it is just as important for you to understand how librarians become aware of books.

Librarians typically order books largely based on reviews. Getting a review into magazines like the following (listed in alphabetical order) can be extremely useful towards awareness exposure into the library markets.

- Booklist (Circulation 80,000 in print; 160,000 online)
- Library Journal (Circulation: 100,000)
- Publishers Weekly (Circulation 68,000)
- School Library Journal (Children/Teen titles) (Circulation: 43,000 in print)
- Voya (YA/Teen Titles – for print and audio)

At the end of this book you will find the URLs for each of these resources along with a bit more information about how to submit to them.

Getting your book listed and/or reviewed in one or more than one of these librarian-centric magazines and online resources can increase the likeliness of the library being aware of and acquiring one or more of your books.

But they are also not easy to get into, and many of them can end up costing you hundreds of dollars, which may take a lot longer for you to earn back.

And, in addition, just having your book listed in such a magazine, journal, or online resource, doesn't mean that there's any guarantee a librarian will actually see it.

So, what does help a librarian find a book?

What other things influence what they might be looking for?

The genre of your book actually makes a huge difference. In general, librarians are constantly looking for commercial fiction in order to appeal to their patrons; and that would include any of the more commercially oriented genres such as romance, and mystery and thriller; science fiction, fantasy, and horror also count among these areas, though the popularity of those genres is often related to what is popular in movies and television, as reader demand in an area often peaks during particular seasons, or trends.

In the height of the *Harry Potter* book and movie release period, for example, there might have been a higher than usual search for young adult fantasy novels. Similarly, when the Peter Jackson movies in the *Lord of the Rings* franchise were released, librarians might have seen more demand for epic fantasy. Dystopian fiction (often considered a sub-genre of science fiction), likely saw growth when *The Hunger Games* books and movies were hot, or with the popularity of *The Handmaid's Tale* television series based on Margaret Atwood's novel of the same name.

Vampire fiction has seen multiple peaks and valleys over the years, from the time when Anne Rice and her *Interview with the Vampire* novels and movie created a larger interest in vampire novels, to the increase in public thirst for vampires and other supernatural beings from Stephanie Meyer's *Twilight* series. If you are writing outside of the commercial genres, this doesn't mean that you can't still find a librarian that would be interested in your titles. That is because every library system, and every branch within each library system, has its own unique patrons, its own preferences, its own staff who each bring something unique.

As mentioned in the bookstore section of this book, each different staff member of a library is going to offer a unique perspective and unique tastes.

Apart from reviews, librarians also acquire books based on customer demand as well as local interest or special collections. That's where being familiar with the trends, such as the examples just mentioned, can come in handy.

If a particular franchise or type of story is popular, epic fantasy, for example, based on Tolkien movies or the popularity of a television series such as *Game of Thrones*, and you have an epic fantasy novel or series that satisfies the cravings of patrons looking for more in that genre, then you have a relatively easy "in" for getting the interest of a librarian.

Beyond popular culture and trends, libraries in different regions might have a unique speciality or flavor to their acquisitions.

Perhaps there is one particular branch, for example, in a city system that specializes in a certain type of book or genre.

Maybe it's a library in a rural area that specializes in books on agriculture; both non-fiction titles or even fiction titles where agriculture is an important element of the fiction. Perhaps it is a branch that focuses on books for children, young readers and teenagers.

Or, to use a specific example of a location that I have visited, there is the Merril Collection branch of the Toronto public library, for example. This location, known as *The Merril Collection of Science Fiction, Speculation & Fantasy* is a non-circulating research collection of 80,000 items of science fiction, fantasy and speculative fiction, as well as magic realism, experimental writing and writing within what are known as the "fringe" areas that include parapsychology, UFOs, ghosts, Atlantean legends, etc.

Understanding a library's area of specialty or regional biases can help you to understand the likeliness of there being a natural fit for your books and their patron community.

But, apart from default preferences and genre trends, librarians do pay close attention to the requests and demands of their patrons.

Basically, librarians often acquire the books their patrons ask them for. They pay close attention to what their local community is interested in, and the books and authors that they specifically request.

That's why I think it's important to focus on the front-line method of reaching out to local libraries.

There are two main ways to do this.

One is by informing your readers (through your author newsletter, or via your social media presence) that your books are available via the library, and actually telling them to go in to their library and request your book. It's actually a great courtesy to your readers and fans of your work. Instead of asking them to purchase your book or books, you're letting them know that they can get access to your book for free, just by asking for the book (in print, eBook, or audiobook format) at their local library. I'll walk through a specific method you can use for that shortly.

The other is by spending the time to get to know your local library and the various branches so that you can properly understand more about them, their preferences, their biases, and their staff.

I would advise a strategy of starting with a library local to your town or city. After all, proximity makes it easier for you to spend time there, which is the best way to witness, first-hand, what that library branch is all about. And then, after you have become comfortable with that, you can do the same thing and move on to the larger country, region, or the state or province.

Start as local as possible, then slowly move your way out. One of the reasons for that isn't just the ease of getting to the local branch for the in person and personal experience. It's for that potential interest in you as a local writer. This can be a significant point of interest for them in general. But also, don't forget to think about the location and setting of your book, whether it's nonfiction or fiction.

Does your novel take place or reference a real world physical location close to where that library is located? Is one of the main characters from a particular area close to that library?

Either of those can be a local interest element.

And that's just another good "in" you can have with a library.

But before you connect with a library, you need to be able to find contact information.

As always, Google is your friend, but sites such as lib-web.org is a fantastic resource that can help you find local libraries in different regions of the world.

I would suggest that you create a spreadsheet of library contact information so you can keep track of the contact info that you have gathered as well as who you've reached out to so you don't have to keep going back to the library website once you find the info that you need.

It's simple if you just stick to local libraries, but it can start to get more complex once you start reaching out to a broader range of library audiences that are beyond your local region.

Your library contact information tracking spreadsheet might be best served with using the following fields:

- Library type (public, academic, public school, etc.)
- Library name
- Library branch
- Website

- Contact name
- Contact title/role
- Email
- Phone number or extension
- Date contacted
- Additional notes

You may have one library where you have multiple contacts, names and titles. So, you might plan on either having multiple contact name, title, email, phone fields, or organize the spreadsheet to contain multiple listings for the same library or branch.

Additional notes might be a field where you keep track of when you heard back from them or perhaps if you hadn't heard back from them, when and how you might want to follow up.

Mining OverDrive for Information

You can also use overdrive.com as a way to find local libraries, which is particularly useful if you're making your books available via OverDrive. It's a little trickier to get to the library's actual website, but overdrive.com does offer a handy map that can be very useful and handy for you to see libraries based on region or postal code or zip code.

Below, I'll walk you through how to use OverDrive to find the specific URLs for your book and your author search result page.

But right now, let's focus on using it to get library contact information.

Once you find a location on the OverDrive map, you can click through it to get to that library's OverDrive specific catalog site. Usually, because it's a default template, if you scroll down to the very bottom, you're likely to find a link to the library's actual website. And it's on that website where you'll be able to find contact information. Unfortunately, every website has their own style, structure and look and feel, so it'll take a bit of browsing around to find what you're looking for.

When looking at library websites, I typically search out three main contacts. They are:

- The acquisitions librarian
- The reference librarian
- The events coordinator

Titles or roles are going to be different in every library system, so you'll have to pay attention to those subtle differences (such as, for example, a reference librarian being referred to as a research librarian); but in essence, the responsibilities of those three roles are what become important.

Not only will different libraries have different ways of naming the roles for these specific people, but in some libraries the roles might be blended together. Larger metropolitan libraries with multiple branches may have head office folks as well as people at different branches that perform similar and overlapping roles. Smaller libraries might just have a few staff members who perform multiple roles; ie, a really small library, where a single librarian is responsible for everything.

In addition, some websites don't list the names of the people in the roles. In those cases, there's often a *Contact Us* form, which you can use to reach out to the libraries.

I have done both. I've reached out directly to specific people with their names and titles and addressed them personally, but I've also used the contact form and mentioned, in my note that my message was intended for the person in charge of acquisitions or special events or perhaps the reference librarian, depending on the context of my message.

Before you reach out, take the time to learn more about the library. Check out their website, see if they have a blog or community newsletter for events or special activity resources. Sign up for and read their newsletter or their blog. Maybe they have videos. Whatever it is that the library offers or specializes is, understand what it is that they're doing and giving to the community, so you have a better feel for who these people are and what they're up to.

And, while this online contact information is extremely useful and important – we do, after all, live in a digital world – it's important to take some time to get into your local library branch or branches, to visit it in person.

A personal visit to the library can provide all kinds of invaluable insights about the library that might never be evident on their website. Get in there and explore it and understand what they do. Attend an event there. Often the special events coordinator or some other person involved in events might be the person introducing the guest speaker or the workshop.

You might even want to visit your local library as a writer with your own writing research needs, and actually work with a reference librarian to do research for your book. That activity makes that librarian intimately familiar with your book while you're creating it. They have a vested interest because they've helped you along the way.

Imagine a librarian talking to a library patron about your book while sharing the fact that you did a portion of your writing and research for it right there in that branch.

Simply, the more familiar you are with the library and their operation, the more comfortable you're going to be when you reach out to them to talk about you and your book and how you and your book can actually serve the library community.

One of the ways you can best serve the library community comes from having all of the information about your book handy prior to your first contact with them as an author telling them about your book. So here's another way you can leverage the information on OverDrive's website.

When you go to overdrive.com and you type in your author name you might see, in the auto-fill drop-down menu that appears there, related search results.

For example, when I type in "Mark Leslie" there are three categories and elements that appear in the drop-down:

Titles
Leslie
Hope Leslie
Leslie's Dilemma
Leslie Fielder
Leslie Ross

Series
Leslie Family
Leslie Frost
Leslie Patricelli Board

Creators
Mark Leslie

It's strange how their search works because "Mark Leslie Lefebvre" the name I use to write my non-fiction books on writing and publishing doesn't appear. If I type in "Mark Leslie Lefebvre" the following appears in the drop-down menu:

Titles
Leslie
Henri Lefebvre
Jules Lefebvre—67 Masterpieces
Henri Lefebvre and Education
Henri Lefebvre on Space

Series
Leslie Family
Leslie Frost
Leslie Patricelli Board

Creators
Mark Leslie
Mark Leslie Lefebvre

If I were to just hit return/enter when typing "Mark Leslie" I would get a search results returned.

www.overdrive.com/search?q=Mark+Leslie

But, if I were to select the "Mark Leslie" that appears in the autofill drop-down menu, I would get:

www.overdrive.com/creators/497001/mark-leslie

Notice the difference between the two. (And this is something you might notice without having to go and look at each page, because the evidence is right in the URL itself) The first is returning a search result (/search?q=Mark+Leslie) and the second one is returning an author landing page (/497001/mark+leslie) which includes a number that is likely like a key identifier to distinguish between one Mark Leslie and another. (There are at least two others that I have seen in online book listings).

The Mark Leslie Lefebvre author page, which is likely to include this book by the time you are reading it, is this.

www.overdrive.com/creators/1789974/mark-leslie-lefebvre

Notice how it ends with */1789974/mark-leslie-lefebvre* which includes a different numeric ID.

The search results page, which is a loose search, is going to return your books as well as other searches. Using the examples above, "Mark Leslie" returns 83 results. Many of them are my books, but there are also others, such as a book co-authored by a "Mark Nichter," another written by "Leslie Butterfield," and one with co-authors by the names of "Mark Avery" and "Roderick Leslie."

So, while the search results page is somewhat useful, the author landing page is one that should contain less "noise." You'll thus want to save your author landing page URL somewhere handy. Perhaps in a tab of the aforementioned library tracking spreadsheet.

When you are looking at your books, either in search results or on your author landing page, you'll notice there are icons in the top left corner that indicate the format of the book. The one that looks like a little open book is for the eBook format. The little headphones icon indicates audiobook.

My chapbook *Snowman Shivers*, for example, which is available in both formats, has both the eBook icon and the audiobook icon.

Snowman Shivers
Mark Leslie (Author)
(2019)

Snowman Shivers
Mark Leslie (Author)
Mark Leslie (Narrator)
(2019)

You might notice, in this example, that the cover dimensions are improperly represented and appear either squished or elongated.

Don't get hung up on that. All books on OverDrive get that auto-reformatted generation, so it's not just your books, it's pretty much every single book there. Librarians are used to that.

In addition, on the right-hand side of the screen you'll see sort options:

Sort
Title
Release Date
˅ Popularity

Notice how Popularity has a symbol indicating it is auto sorted by most popular to least popular. Clicking on it will toggle it to ˆ which is least popular to most popular.

You'll also see filtering options:

Filter
> Subjects
> Publisher
> Media type
> Format

Beneath each of these are a tally of the number of options. For example, under subject, at the time I am looking at this page, there are 8 different subjects. The subjects are sorted by the most populous. For "Mark Leslie" there are Fiction (33), Horror (22), Short Stories (21), Fantasy (10), etc.

Under Publisher, in the same example, there are 8 options. Stark Publishing (26), Dundurn (9), WMG Publishing Incorporated (4), etc. These are examples of two traditional publishers I work with and my own imprint.

Media type, in my case, shows the two main types of eBook (35) and Audiobook (8).

And, finally, Format for my books reveal 6 options which are: Adobe EPUB eBook (34), OverDrive Read (33), Kindle Book (11), OverDrive MP3 Audiobook (8), OverDrive Listen (8), Open EPUB Book (1).

Other Filters that might appear include Language, Release Date, and Creators.

Librarians can use any of these filtering options when looking for books, but you are going to want to make a note of the unique URLs to help save them the time of doing any searching.

Using the examples of my short collection **Snowman Shivers**, below are the URLs for the eBook:

www.overdrive.com/media/4882344/snowman-shivers

...and for the audiobook...

www.overdrive.com/media/4998142/snowman-shivers

Similar to the author landing page, notice that each one of these has a unique numeric ID. This is the unique to OverDrive identifier. Think of it like their internal ISBN that they use for tracking and storing your book.

Make a note of these URLs.

Finally, on the OverDrive website, have a look at the digital stock for the books. This is where you can determine whether or not a particular library or branch has acquired stock of one of your titles.

On the item detail page for your book you'll see two large buttons that read:

- FIND in your library
- In libraries nearby

You either have to be logged in (with library defaults set), or allow the computer to show your location, or you can type in the name of your city or another city, and you can see an indication of various locations that might have stock of your title.

If I look up my book *The 7 P's of Publishing Success* for example, I can see all the branch locations of the Waterloo Public Library and Kitchener Public Library that have stock. When I click on one of those branches, at the time of this writing, I can see that there are 0 of 1 copies available in Kitchener/Waterloo for that book. This means that that library system purchased 1 copy and that, at this time, that copy is checked out and being read by a patron.

For my traditionally published book *Haunted Hospitals* co-authored with Rhonda Parrish, I can see that Waterloo Public Library and Kitchener Public Library each have 0 copies available (meaning they haven't purchased it at this time), Hamilton Public Library has 1 of 1 copies available, and Toronto Public Library has 2 of 2 copies available.

You can follow the link directly to any of the books that are already available and let patrons know that they can get them.

For example, here is a tweet that I sent out in November 2019 linking to my book at the shared download resources of Waterloo Public Library and Kitchener Public Library.

Are you participating in #NaNoWriMo? Looking for tips on long term writer success? My book The 7 P's of Publish Success is avail in print, eBook & audio. You can read the eBook for free via @KitchLibrary or @WaterlooLibrary [LINK]

Mark Leslie Lefebvre @MarkLeslie   2m
Are you participating in #NaNoWriMo?
Looking for tips on long term writer
success? My book The 7 P's of Publishing
Success is avail in print, eBook & audio.
You can read the eBook for free via
@KitchLibrary or @WaterlooLibrary
downloadlibrary.overdrive.com/media
/7d4560fe...

Based on this research on you and your books, you might want to create a unique tab in the aforementioned spreadsheet that hosts your book information, and for each book include such fields as:

- Book title
- Format
- Author
- Narrator
- USD Price
- In OverDrive catalog (Y/N)
- OverDrive URL
- In Library Stock at
- Library Stock URL

The "In Library Stock at" field is likely to be used multiple times, depending on how you format the spreadsheet, and in conjunction with the "Library Stock URL" field. For example:

- In Library Stock at 1
- Library Stock URL 1
- In Library Stock at 2
- Library Stock URL 2
- In Library Stock at 3
- Library Stock URL 3

Reaching Out to The Library

Now that you have done your homework and learned more about your local library or particular libraries where there is a connection to you and your writing, and you have also found and captured information about your book or books, it's time to reach out to libraries.

As you consider reaching out, make sure to keep the following things in mind.

How do you and your book serve library community? What is the uniqueness that either you or your book offer to that particular library?

If you simply reach out blind to a local library with a "Dear Sirs" style letter that talks about why your book is great and why they should carry your book, you may not get the same reception as reaching out to a local branch where you've already attended an event and you can even comment on, or compliment them on something about their library.

I like to follow a basic structure for reaching out and contacting libraries:

- Point 1: You & your library are awesome
- Point 2: Me and my book are awesome
- Point 3: Here is an awesome thing that me and my book can offer your awesome library

That's a bit of a hyperbole, but remember, people are always quite interested in themselves, so start with something about them.

Then briefly introduce you and what you're about (keeping in mind how it might relate to them), and end with something unique that you can offer them. You can also include some of your experience that helps highlight the offer.

This isn't a sales pitch – it's a note about what you might have that can help them or make their lives easier by assisting with an offering to their patrons.

Here's an example of the type of letter that might work, addressed to a specific person, in this case the person who oversees events at the main library branch.

Dear Sheila:

I attended the Kitchener Public Library book launch for James Allen Gardener last month, and I had a wonderful time. The event in your stunning atrium was informative and inspiring, and I particularly loved the

Q&A interview format with James that made it feel like James was a guest on a late night talk show.

I'm an author who recently moved to the region and I have recently published a book for writers that is available in print, eBook and audiobook. The ISBNs for each format are listed below, as is a link to the book via OverDrive where you can see the eBook and the audiobook versions.

I offer workshops that help writers understand the business of writing and publishing, and I would love the opportunity to discuss hosting a workshop for any of your patrons who may be interested in getting started in writing, or perhaps in furthering their knowledge and understanding of the business aspects of writing and publishing.

Apart from the aforementioned book, I've written or edited more than 20 books in the past 15 years with small presses, with Dundurn Press, Canada's largest domestic publisher, as well as indie published titles. I have also worked in the book industry since 1992.

I would love to discuss leveraging my experience to help with any writing and publishing programming needs that you have, and I look forward to connecting with you.

Sincerely,

Mark Leslie Lefebvre

The letter would include the ISBNs for each format, the URLs to the books mentioned in OverDrive's catalog, perhaps also the URL to my OverDrive author page, as well as my full contact information, including phone number.

Remember, the key is to be concise, polite and as specific as possible about your book and about how you and your book might serve the library community.

And, of course, following a style that it suitable for you.

I think it's important, when you're talking to the library, to ensure they know you're familiar with them. If you've had a good experience in any way with the library share it with them. It doesn't matter if it's about something on their website, like an article, or blog post or staff recommendation element; maybe it was something in their monthly newsletter; or perhaps it was an event or even some sort of curation that they've done for a book that was recommended to you.

It doesn't matter what it is. Take the time to let them know that you appreciate what they're doing in and for the community. Let them know that you're a part of this community. And then let them know what it is that you can do to help them in something that they do to serve the community; that you're there to provide them with valuable content and resources in that mission.

Because that's what a library is. A library is valuable content, valuable resources.

In terms of who to contact at the library, if I don't already know specific people from my own visits – ie, if the contact being made is mostly due to online research, I try to reach out to the three main contact people that I've mentioned earlier in this chapter.

The Acquisitions Librarian

The acquisitions or the collections librarians are typically the ones who do the purchasing. It makes sense to contact them when letting them know about your new or your backlist book.

When you are reaching out to the acquisitions librarian it is useful if you understand and express how the book you are pitching to them fulfills a particular need for the library patron.

This goes back to the core fundamental of having fully fleshed out your target audience by knowing what comparable titles your book will appeal to. And, the bigger name the author, the more likely you are to get the attention of the librarian.

This is because, with limited budgets, and with the significant costs that most major publishers charge libraries for eBooks (usually anywhere between $30 and $80 per copy, and, often with a limited term), there might be an opportunity for your books to fulfill an important library need.

Let's take a look at, what to me, is a very obvious example.

Lee Child is the author of the Jack Reacher novels. Reacher is a character who is widely known and loved (you might recognize him as being played by Tom Cruise in a series of movies), and, for avid thriller readers, and, in particular, librarians, Lee Child is a well-known name.

Independently published author Diane Capri, who happens to be good friends with Child, has a number of novels in the *The HUNT FOR REACHER Series* which are the only official authorized Reacher novels. These books are also recommended by Lee Child. In her agreement with Child, Capri doesn't have Reacher actually appear in her books; he is never explicitly seen in them. The series features FBI agents who are on the trail of Reacher, and appear in each of the locales he has recently visited.

The first novel in her series, ***Don't Know Jack*** takes place in Margrave, Georgia, fifteen years after Reacher appeared there in Child's first Reacher novel ***Killing Floor***. The other novels follow the agents as they continue to track Reacher's "off the grid" wandering.

For readers who can't get enough Reacher stories and are all caught up on the books by Child, or even for the readers who are on the long waiting lists for the latest Lee Child novels at most library systems, these novels by Capri fulfill an important demand.

A sample pitch to a library would likely include the details mentioned above, as well as one of the many positive review quotes that Lee Child has provided about the books.

In looking at the latest Jack Reacher novel ***Blue Moon***, which is book 24 in the series and which was released October 29, 2019, in early November of 2019, here are some examples of the number of copies available and the estimated wait times on them from three of the largest library networks near where I live:

- **Waterloo Public Library**: 0 of 4 copies are available with a wait time of at least 6 months
- **Hamilton Public Library**: 0 of 9 copies are available with a wait time of at least 6 months
- **Toronto Public Library**: 0 of 80 copies are available with a wait time of about 13 weeks

But what about other major Canadian and US cities?

- **New York Public Library**: 0 of 67 copies are available with a wait time of about 16 weeks
- **Los Angeles Public Library**: 0 of 261 copies are available with a wait time of about 5 weeks
- **Chicago Public Library**: 0 of 20 copies are available with a wait time of about 16 weeks
- **Vancouver Public Library**: 0 of 9 copies are available with a wait time of at least 6 months
- **Halifax Public Library**: 0 of 9 copies are available with a wait time of at least 6 months
- **Montreal (Bibliothèques des banlieues de l'Île de Montréal)**: 0 of 1 copies are available with a wait time of at least 6 months

I'm not sure how you interpret those numbers, but I would say that this is a prime opportunity for an author like Diane Capri, whose novels have a direct tie-in to the Jack Reacher universe, to help those libraries with satisfying their patrons needs.

And, based on the more reasonable price that I know Capri sets for libraries, a library could likely acquire all twelve of her *The Hunt For Reacher Series* novels for the price of perhaps two or three copies of the novels by Lee Child, easily satisfying plenty of library patrons looking for a good read that is right in their wheelhouse.

Other authors, who have characters and a series that are similar in style to Lee Child's Jack Reacher would likely also do well with a similar approach.

UK bestselling author Mark Dawson, who writes a series of a Reacher-like character named John Milton, would do well in this environment. Of course, at the time of this writing, most of Dawson's Milton books are exclusive to Amazon Kindle via KDP Select, which means that, while he is earning a significant amount of money from Amazon, that particular IP is not available for library patrons, or for taking advantage of such an opportunity within libraries.

For print books, you can sometimes see not only how many copies are in stock, but also how many holds might be on a book. I remember, for example, looking at a listing for my book **Haunted Hamilton** when it first came out in the online catalog of the Hamilton Public Library, and seeing that all the copies the library had owned were checked out, and that there were more than 300 people with the book on hold.

I remember it because two things stuck out: First, I was both surprised and impressed that the library had purchased numerous copies; second, that there were that many people interested in it. I suppose I shouldn't have been surprised; I had, after all, appeared on the local morning television program, CHCH, talking about the new book; and a couple of local newspapers had featured positive reviews of the book.

But this information about what is popular and on demand in print is also useful information that you can use as an author to determine a library's patron activity.

Browsing on the Hamilton Public Library site, I can browse over to the Bestsellers list, where they have listed bestsellers according to four different criteria:

- CANADA: Canadian Independent Booksellers
- CANADA: Globe and Mail
- UNITED STATES: Indie Bestsellers (USA)*
- UNITED STATES: New York Times

* *Please note, if you're a self-published/indie author, don't get too excited about the term "Indie Bestsellers" – Indie is a term that independently owned bookstores have been using for decades before authors came along and adapted the term for their own use. Sorry, they don't mean bestselling indie published books, they mean the bestselling books as reported by indie bookstores.*

You can use the bestseller status at the independent bookstores to determine the overall popularity of titles in indie bookstores, and this is useful; but it's important to remember that this is a blended result across a large number of stores, each with their own unique customer base. Regional and local variances are huge.

But these bestsellers lists are a great way to gage the popularity of books, and in multiple formats.

For example, one of the books at the top of the list is Margaret Atwood's **The Handmaid's Tale**.

- **Print Book**: *All copies in use.*
  o   Holds: 29 on 45 copies
- **eBook**: *All copies in use.*
  o   Holds: 55 on 27 copies
- **Audiobook CD**: *All copies in use.*
  o   Holds: 10 on 4 copies
- **Large Print**: *All copies in use.*
  o   Holds: 8 on 11 copies

If you had a dystopian novel, or perhaps a novel that involves a stark look at the roles of women in society, it appears that there's likely a potential for your book to help that library fulfill a particular demand. Yes, I'm aware that the demand is likely due to the popular television show (and likely students needing to read the text for a university or college course), but some of that demand will overflow to readers who'll be interested. And there'll also be the folks who have read both this novel and Atwood's follow-up novel and might be looking for something more.

Looking at Michael Connelly's **The Night Fire**, which was just released a couple of weeks ago at the time of this writing, I can see the following.

- **Print Book**: *All copies in use.*

o   Holds: 220 on 35 copies
- **Audiobook CD**: *All copies in use.*
  o   Holds: 31 on 4 copies
- **Large Print**: *All copies in use.*
  o   Holds: 42 on 4 copies

Do you have a police procedural? Maybe even a series of a police procedural? That might fit.

Also, because this is part of a newer series that features Detective Rene Ballard, a newer character, who has teamed up with retired Detective Harry Bosch, there could be a great appeal for an author like Carolyn Arnold.

Arnold, who lives in London, Ontario, has adopted the trademark: *POLICE PROCEDURALS RESPECTED BY LAW ENFORCEMENT*™ and has four continuing series that include cozy mysteries, hard-boiled mysteries, thrillers, and action adventures.

But her Detective Madison Knight series is likely one that would appeal to readers of this Bosch/Ballard novel and series.

On top of that, Arnold is an author who lives in London, Ontario. A quick look at the London Public Library reveals the following about Connelly's latest novel:

- **Print Book**: *Not available.*
  o   225 holds on first copy returned of 30 copies
- **Large Print**: *Not available.*
  o   58 holds on first copy returned of 5 copies

- **Audiobook CD**: *Not available.*
  - o 14 holds on first copy returned of 4 copies
- **E-Audio**: *Not available.*
  - o 0 of 3 copies available. 41 on hold
- **eBook**: *Not available.*
  - o 0 of 8 copies available. 62 on hold

To me, this seems like a ripe opportunity for a local author like Carolyn Arnold to leverage. Because, not only would knowing about and having her books in multiple formats provide a similar reading experience to what the readers get from Connelly, but there's also the "local author" angle that some librarians might enjoy showcasing.

I can imagine a librarian, having to tell countless customers each day that the hot new Connelly novel is on hold, and that the wait time is likely more than a few weeks, "but we do have stock of an internationally bestselling local author by the name of Carolyn Arnold who has a fantastic police procedural that has been described as respected by law enforcement. Would you like me to show them to you?"

I'm hoping that sharing these examples gives you an idea of how you might be able to leverage this for your own purposes.

The key is to know who your readers are, what other books; especially the more popular books and authors and series, your readers are likely to enjoy, and see if there is a way that you and your books can fulfill those needs.

That is what is important to make sure you share with the acquisitions librarian.

An Important Cautionary Note: Whatever you do, **do not** attempt to compare your book in style or content, to a major author if there is no close match, merely because the author is well-known and popular. That will only serve to highlight you as both unprofessional and unreliable.

There is an obvious and direct relation between the novels Diane Capri has written and the popular Lee Child novels. Or between the police procedurals that Carolyn Arnold writes and most of Michael Connelly's novels.

But if Capri were to suggest that her novels would appeal to readers of J.K. Rowling's *Harry Potter* series, or Arnold were to suggest her novel **Christmas is Murder** in her cozy McKinley Mysteries series would be perfect for Connelly's police procedural readers, that would be misleading.

Sometimes it can be helpful to also reach out to the other roles mentioned before, such as the events coordinator or the reference librarian, which I will get to a little later.

But you also might want to ensure that the director or the head librarian or the branch manager also knows about it too, because it never hurts to have more than one person made aware of your book.

Here's one of the reasons it's good to try to establish contact with more than one person. Perhaps the acquisitions person doesn't like the type of book that you write; or maybe they just received your information on a bad day; such as a day where they were short staffed and had to cover someone else's role, and they received twice as many emails as normal that day, and ended up skipping through half of them, including yours, without really attending to it.

But perhaps the head librarian at that branch is a huge fan of the type of book you are pitching. Or maybe one of the other folks working in a different area of the library resonates with you or your book. It's not all that different from the way that different booksellers in the same store might react differently to you and your book or books.

Connecting with them can make all the difference.

Different librarians have different tastes and different approaches and different styles, and so being in contact with different people at the library or even establishing relationships with them in an authentic and real way could actually work out in your favor in the long run.

Mark Leslie Lefebvre

The Events Librarian

Reaching out to the librarian who oversees events is typically done when you are offering to fulfill some sort of event.

In my own case, because I have written a number of true ghost story books, letting the library know that I am available to do a talk about local history and local ghosts, and making that offer in mid to late summer (about the time they are looking at scheduling their October events, usually events that include a Halloween theme) works well.

I have, of course, done historic ghost talks in the middle of the winter, too. But I have found that the interest in that topic peaks during the lead in to Halloween.

In general, readings on their own don't necessarily work well – except, perhaps, for readings of picture books to younger children. This may be because many authors aren't skilled at readings, or they might go on too long, which can lead to patron unrest. I have found that doing a very brief reading, to give the audience a flavor of the book, combined with a talk related to the book or story, works best.

This is where you have to apply the same creativity that you would have applied to writing your book.

It's easy for me to derive content for a talk about local ghosts; but what if it's a novel, rather than a non-fiction book about that city?

Does anything related to your book or writing connect to a workshop or presentation that you can do at the local library? How about the journey of writing and publishing your book?

I have done workshops on how to write scary stories. I have also done workshops on how to write query letters to publishers, how to self-publish an eBook, how to perform research for a novel. All of these were derived from my own experience as a writer.

Canadian bestselling author Terry Fallis does an amazing talk on his unorthodox journey through publishing, sharing how, when he wasn't able to find a publisher, he self-published the book and began podcasting his novel for free and gained a world-wide audience; then, how his self-published novel won a major literary award, which landed him an agent, a publishing deal, which led to more than seven other novels plus a television show based on his first novel – the same one that publishers weren't, at first, interested in.

What is unique or interesting about your own author journey that could intrigue or inspire the patrons of a library who are fascinated with writing?

Perhaps there's something inspiring from the research you had to do. Perhaps the hook from the premise of your novel is something that can draw a reader's attention.

Years ago, I was interviewing UK author Peter James in front of a bookish audience. He ended up sharing stories of how one of his early readers was a police detective who had reached out to correct him on an error he had inserted into his novel. James relayed the tale of how he thanked the man for helping him identify a logistical error to correct and then asked if he would read the early draft of his next book in case a similar error or misperception appeared. The man was honored to be asked, eagerly read and provided feedback on the novel, and a long-term friendship resulted from that experience.

Michael Connelly, whom I interviewed in a similar fashion, also relayed stories about the relationships he has had with law enforcement professionals over the years, as well as his own background as a crime reporter before he penned his first police procedural crime thriller.

Canadian science fiction author Robert J. Sawyer is a genius at relaying the premise for so many of his novels that usually combine a speculation based on real science combined with a brief "what if" that make for fascinating talks.

For his novel *Flashforward*, for example, which was adapted into an ABC television series, the basic premise was: *If you could see the future, would you be able to change it?* This premise came from a casual conversation that took place during a high school reunion. In the story, an experiment with The Large Hadron Collider (the world's largest and most powerful particle accelerator) leads everyone in the world to blackout for about two minutes where they have a short vision of their future.

In Sawyer's *WWW* trilogy of *Wake*, *Watch*, and *Wonder* his premise was: *Given that the world wide web is expected, by the early 21st century, to have the same number of synapses as the human brain, what if, like the human brain, it developed a consciousness?* That came from a combination of an article from *New Scientist,* Sawyer's fascination with chimpanzee sign-language, the nature of perception, and a reimagination of the relationship between Helen Keller and her teacher, Anne Sullivan.

Without even getting into the details of the plot of either of these novels, Sawyer can hold an audience in rapt fascination, wonder, and speculation just talking about the premises.

So, in that same manner, what, in the genesis of your own novel, inspired you to write it? What about the research that you did for it could be an interesting tale to share? Is there an aspect of the book based on the setting that could be of interest to that local audience? Is there a classic book or movie that relates to your book; or perhaps a combination of two potentially disparate ones? How did you go about the research for your book, and where did you find the information that you needed? What deeply important personal experience led you to writing this novel, or non-fiction or self-help book?

If nothing from those questions work, you can always draw from the experience of writing the book. Often, beginning writers can be fascinated with learning more about the behind-the-scenes of a writer's life. Where did your original idea for the book come from? And how did you adapt that initial idea into the construct of the book? Are you a *pantser* or a *plotter*, or some combination of the two? What sort of environment best suits your writing – quiet isolation, or the hustle and bustle of a busy coffee shop? Do you listen to music when you write – and do different genres or styles of music suit different types of your writing? How much of your personal experience is baked into the various characters in your novels?

The key is that there are likely plenty of things you can talk about and share about your book that are derived from the content, subject matter, or theme from the book. And while none of those involves an author reading from the text of the book, plenty of them are wider reaching generic subjects that might be interesting to an events librarian looking for content to entertain or inform their patrons.

The Reference Librarian

Contacting the reference librarian can also be critical. Reference librarians are amazing folks and are an incredible community resource. These are the folks who often oversee the main information and archives or resource and research desk in the library. They are typically beautiful data nerds who love collecting and gathering and storing and sharing information.

Their role is to collect and to give out information. Ensuring that they know about you, that you're a local author, perhaps that you're a subject matter expert in a particular area, or a genre author of a specific niche, is likely something they're going to file away and that they may pull out for the appropriate local researcher who comes along.

Like in other more in-depth strategies for authors, it's not a tactic, but rather a long-term investment that you are making in your career.

In my own writing journey, I have spent countless hours with different reference librarians when researching for my nonfiction books about ghosts. For example, when I was doing research for my book *Haunted Hamilton,* I spent a significant amount of time at the main branch of the Hamilton Public Library where Margaret Houghton, who was the local public library archivist at the time, tirelessly filled me with all kinds of information about local history; and, in particular, local ghostly tales.

She gave me access to a wonderful file folder of newspaper clippings, historical articles, and other collected documents that were all related to ghosts and the paranormal and the darker aspects of Hamilton's past. This special file, in the back of the local archives section, is information that I would not have known about or had access to using any of their online systems or even any of the great online resources for the library.

It was through in-person discussions and conversation about the book I was researching for that I learned about all these things. Margaret, who has been described as Hamilton's most beloved chronicler of local history, was amazingly helpful. And I'm pretty sure that up until her retirement in 2016 she very likely put my book *Haunted Hamilton* into the hands of countless potential readers who came in and were looking for spookier and darker tales of the city; because that's the kind of thing that a reference librarian does.

So even if the acquisitions person might not be interested in your book, or you don't get any nibbles on events that you have offered to the library, sometimes the local archivist or the reference librarian knowing about you, knowing about your book, may be something that they can recommend to different consumers who come in there.

During the school year, for example, children regularly show up at the library and say that their teacher wants them to read a Canadian author. Or their teacher says they have to read an author from their home state of Nebraska. Or a book set in the particular county or region native to the school. Can the library recommend a book? It's usually the reference librarian who is interested in collecting and storing this type of information and they often love having those answers either at the ready, or within their archives of data.

Returning to Robert J. Sawyer, since the aforementioned *Wake, Watch, Wonder* trilogy or novels were primarily set in Waterloo and involve the main character's father working at Waterloo's Perimeter Institute for Theoretical Physics, the books have a local hook that could be compelling for local reference librarians in my locale of Kitchener, Waterloo, and Cambridge. And James Alan Gardner, a local Kitchener-Waterloo based author I mentioned in the chapter on bookselling (his "local author" status is already a hook for Waterloo Region librarians), set his two most recent novels, *All Those Explosions Were Someone Else's Fault* and *They Promised Me The Gun Wasn't Loaded* in the area, with his main characters being students (and superheroes) at the University of Waterloo.

Context, content, and contributor are three things that a reference librarian values; particularly how each of those elements relates to their particular local library needs.

The Library's Needs

To summarize a common element that flows through the contacts that you have with the library, your focus should always be on how you and your book(s) are able to fulfill a need they have in serving the local community. Whether it's information, inspiration, insight, or just plain entertainment, there is likely something that you are able to offer that might be of value to the library.

Think of it the same way that pundits recommend you engage in your social media strategy. It's an 80% give and share, and 20% ask or request. And if you have to lean or default in any way, make that split a 90 / 10 split, always heavy on the side of providing value and content.

You want the people who manage and work at the library to see their relationship with you as a benefit, not a burden.

Additional Context & Background

One of the main reasons why I suggest, when contacting a library to let them know about your books, that you include links to the books in OverDrive, is because of something that happened relatively early on in the digital book revolution.

Smashwords, the first major free-to-use and author-centric eBook distribution platform, which was founded in 2008, was also the first to allow independently published authors an opportunity to get their works into libraries, through 3M's Bibliotheca and OverDrive.

In the spring of 2014, when *Smashwords* first announced an agreement to provide OverDrive with more than 200,000 titles, librarians were delighted with access to an entirely new catalog of books that were priced incredibly lower than prices they had ever seen before.

At first, the librarians were enthusiastic with the pricing because after all, the major publishers were charging ridiculously high rates for their books. Major publishers charge upwards of between thirty dollars and eighty dollars for a single title. But libraries could suddenly buy ten or even a dozen books from *Smashwords* for the price of a single hot title from a major publisher.

Unfortunately, that enthusiasm, that delight, went south rather quickly.

Because that initial flooding of the OverDrive database came without any sort of curation. And librarians love curation.

But what happened, particularly since *Smashwords* uses an automatic "opt-in" process, was that everything was automatically opted in.

In fact, if you read the announcement on the *Smashwords* website about acquisitions, 100,000 titles had already been automatically opted in and sent to libraries before *Smashwords* authors even knew about it.

This resulted in a significant number of incredibly crappy, unedited dregs from the self-publishing world overwhelming a previously tightly curated catalog of titles from major publishers.

If you are a self-published author, please don't take this the wrong way. I know that a properly written, edited and polished indie published book is indistinguishable from a book from the world's largest publisher. In fact, in many cases, I actually default to thinking that they are superior in many ways. But the stark reality is that there are tens of thousands of completely horrible, unedited and hastily slapped-together books that are also released every day.

This is, of course, one side-effect of the removal of the gatekeepers. Everyone can publish. Which means that absolutely *everyone* can publish. The talented writers who work hard at their craft and who work at producing the best books they can no longer have to wait for the gatekeepers sitting in expensive offices in New York city to grant their approval; but this, in effect, means that anyone else, without proper research, without proper editing, without any sort of professional approach, has that same access to publish.

Smashwords was, of course, the first major presence to make this a reality for authors. And please don't get me wrong. I admire Mark Coker, the founder and CEO of *Smashwords*, and consider him a pioneer who was at the forefront of this amazing evolution in the publishing industry for authors. *Smashwords* was the first major free eBook publishing platform that could help authors get their books listed on all the major retailers. Tens of thousands of authors whose dream of seeing their book published got to realize that dream.

This is, in no way, something I would ever purposely undermine. As an author who signed up with them early on, I am thankful for *Smashwords*, for their role in helping to lead this charge, for their dedication to helping remove the gatekeepers of traditional publishing from the paths of so many writers. But I also have to recognize that, with that same removal of limitations, there would also be a flow of unfiltered dreck.

And, in this case, the gatekeeping, or curation, into a massive library wholesaler catalog, was also removed.

In this flood of titles, the crappy and unedited books were sent right alongside everything else. They were just as prominent as the highly polished, the professionally edited, the amazing and stellar indie titles.

There was no curation, no top-selling list that came along with that. No hand-selected recommendations based on any sort of criteria.

Just a flood of noise.

Librarians ended up wasting their time and money on so much dreck because they were flooded with hundreds of thousands of titles.

This meant that those stellar and bestselling titles and the crappy unedited books were mixed in together and there really was no easy way to tell the difference.

Or, at least there was no easy way to tell the difference until it was too late and plenty of libraries had wasted their money and, perhaps more importantly, they'd wasted their time.

This is a case where the unwashed masses created a bad name for indie or self-published titles in the eyes of librarians, or perhaps they reaffirmed a previously held belief that librarians had about self published titles.

In either case, it needed to be addressed.

Because there were, and continue to be, librarians who are interested in knowing about or carrying self-published titles. They just needed a good way of finding them, and, ideally, some sort of way to sort the wheat from the chaff.

Because OverDrive is a company that offers amazing Business-to-Business service – they respect their library customers and want to make things easier for them – they had to implement a solution.

And they had to implement it rather quickly to make up for the angst that had been caused.

OverDrive split their catalog into two.

The one half is their main regular catalog that all libraries use by default, and it is filled with titles from the major publishers, Penguin Random House, Harper Collins, Macmillan, Simon and Schuster, and others that would include smaller presses, like one of my publishers, Dundurn Press, Canada's largest independent publisher.

The other catalog, or the other partition of the catalog is perhaps the equivalent of the OverDrive ghetto, and it's populated with all of the self-published titles from all the various sources for self-published titles. This includes *Smashwords*, *Draft2Digital*, *StreetLib*, *PublishDrive*, *BookBaby*, even *Kobo Writing Life*, OverDrive's sister company.

Therefore, when a librarian checks the OverDrive catalog for a book, by habit or default, they immediately go to the main database that they have always used. Some librarians might not even think to look at the secondary catalog of titles. And some others, particularly those that might have had a bad experience with it in the early days, might purposely not look at it.

Consider the way that you might search things.

Let's assume that you often use Google search, because that's what you've always done. It'd be like wanting to look something up and using Google to search something and not finding what you were looking for. You might try a few variations of the search term or phrase you're using, but if you come up without finding what you had been looking for, do you consider trying another online search engine, or do you just stop, thinking that if the world's most prominent search engine doesn't have it, it likely doesn't exist.

When you're getting a librarian to search OverDrive for your book, you don't want them giving up if they don't find it in the main database.

Showing them that it exists, via a URL link to the book in OverDrive's catalog, is one way to help overcome that small hump in the process on their end.

That's why sending the librarian as much information as you can is important. The ISBN, the link to the book in OverDrive's catalog that includes that OverDrive ID can make a difference. This shows them that your book is indeed available in the OverDrive catalog, which means if they don't at first see it, they'll know to keep looking in the secondary catalog.

And yes, that secondary search might come with some preconceived bias on their part, but if your communication and your relationship with the library is professional and respectful, and if they believe that you or your book are going to bring value to them and their patrons, then they're more likely to give you and your book the benefit of the potential doubt.

Another way of building awareness and assisting with acquisition to libraries is leveraging your fan base and people in your community. If you have a newsletter, a website, social media, or other ways to communicate with fans and you're announcing your new book, don't forget to let them know that the book is also available to the public library.

Draft2Digital's free Books2Read universal book link, for example, shows the OverDrive link, which means that people you go to that page can not only see the icon for their favorite retailer, but then they can also click on the link to OverDrive, which can lead them to their local library.

Be sure to let your fans know that they can read virtually any one of your books that you make available through the library systems for free by asking for it at their own local library.

Fans who do this are actually doing you a favor when they ask, because when a library receives a request from a patron it has real meaning to them. They exist to serve their patrons, and they pay close attention to the books and types of requests that patrons make.

The request from someone in their community might inspire them to want to carry that book, and it is likely even more effective than hearing from the author themselves.

Although learning about the book from an author, and, in particular, if the author shares a useful hook for that library, whether it is a "local author" or "local setting" or how a book might appeal to a specific demographic of readers, combined with patron requests can be ultimately effective.

In addition, I have to share another important note that might be specifically useful to authors who, prior to publishing "wide" to all retailers and libraries, had their books in Amazon's *KDP Select* exclusivity program, which puts their books into Amazon's Kinde Unlimited program of "all you can read" for a monthly fee.

Sometimes, particularly if an author has built their platform leveraging those "free reads" via Kindle Unlimited, they can get push-back from some of their fans.

Some very vocal Kindle Unlimited readers might be angry and contact you and complain that, at one time, there were able to read all your books for free because your books were part of Kindle Unlimited. But now that they're not, they can't get your books for free, and therefore will not read your books, or give you one star reviews.

First of all, I know that KU is not really free because the customer is paying Amazon a monthly or annual fee to be part of the Kindle Unlimited program; but the appearance is that that they're reading it for free because they get unlimited reading as part of that program.

I think that a really good answer to a person who complains to you about this is letting them know that your book is still available for free not just to a limited number of Amazon customers but also to millions more potential readers around the world and that you did this because you want more people to be able to read your books for free and not have to pay a single dime. Because now everyone can get the book free via their local library. And, with that communication, provide the link to where they can now still access the book for free. OverDrive has a great free reading app named Libby that people can download to their smartphones. And many of the newer Kobo readers have a built-in functionality that hooks up directly to OverDrive's catalog; which means they can borrow the book from their local library without ever even having to step away from their Kobo eBook reader.

So, you not only have an answer to those readers who want it for free, but you're letting them know that your recent adjustment is allowing more people access to your writing.

Yes, I know that there will be selfish people who don't want to change or do anything differently, and you might just lose those readers. There will always be naysayers and those who choose to be angry rather than accept a solution outside of their existing perspectives or biases. But true fans who perhaps can't afford to buy a lot of books can follow you and still read one of their favorite authors for free.

When I have shared this "you can read it at the library for free" from the stage or in online forums, there's always some wise guy in the crowd who comments that libraries aren't free, they are paid for via taxes.

Yes, I get it. I know. Like roads, sidewalks, highways, running water and garbage collection and other infrastructure items, funding for libraries is often derived from local, county, state, provincial, and federal taxes.

But in the same way that people pay a giant corporation, Amazon to "read for free" via Kindle Unlimited, perhaps you can throw me a bone and accept that, to the average library patron, the reading is pretty much free.

So, by letting your readers know they can also get the book at the library by asking for your book in their own community where they can read it for free, they're actually also helping you.

And your readers do often want to help an author that they like.

Why Indie Authors Are More Relevant to Libraries Than Ever Before

We have already explored how your books can be considered comparable to titles from big-name or household authors.

We have already delved into pricing strategies that allow you to be competitive in a very cut-throat landscape.

But something happened in mid to late 2019 that allowed the playing ground to shift yet again. And it's something you need to be aware of so you can leverage that to your advantage.

Because the ground shifted in a positive way for indie authors.

In July 0f 2018, Macmillan Publishers, an international publishing company owned by Holtzbrink Publishing Group, used *Tor Books* their leading science-fiction publishing imprint, as part of an experiment to assess the impact of library eBook lending on retail sales. Newly released titles under that imprint were no longer available for library sales until four months after their retail sales date.

After a full year of this experiment, which ReadersFirst, a coalition of 300 libraries dedicated to improving eBook access and services for public library users considered a giant leap backwards, Macmillan announced that, starting November 1, 2019, it would impose a two-month embargo on library eBooks across all of the company's imprints.

Below is a quote from a July 25, 2019 article by Andrew Albanese in *Publisher's Weekly*.

> Under the publisher's new digital terms of sale for libraries, "library systems" will now be allowed to purchase a single—that is, *one*—perpetual access e-book during the first eight weeks of publication for each new Macmillan release, at half price ($30). Additional copies will then be available at full price (generally $60 for new releases) after the eight-week window has passed. All other terms remain the same: e-book licenses will continue to be metered for two years or 52 lends, whichever comes first, on a one copy/one user model. A Macmillan spokesperson confirmed to *PW* that the single perpetual access copy will be available only for new release titles in the first eight weeks after publication—the option to buy a single perpetual access copy expires after that eight week window, and the offer is not available for backlist titles.

As of the writing of this book, the same embargo hasn't yet happened on audiobooks – yet.

But I see this as a major opportunity for independently published authors. You can likely leverage this to your advantage, first, by making your eBooks available to the libraries for a reasonable and competitive price, and, second, by doing a bit of research and ensuring you are familiar with some of the larger, more house-hold name authors whose hot new *New York Times* bestseller titles are limited in availability for two months.

Chances are that there is huge demand in libraries for these titles. And if you have published a book that would appeal to these same readers, you are in luck. Because you are likely able to offer the library a way to satisfy some of the hunger from those readers who are likely on a huge waiting list.

So, as part of your library strategy, it might make sense to take the time to investigate the new and forthcoming releases from the various Macmillan imprints, looking for titles and authors that your books are likely to appeal to.

The Macmillan imprints currently include:

- Celadon Books
- Farrar, Straus and Giroux
- Picador
- North Point Press
- Hill and Wang
- Henry Holt and Company
- Times Books
- Roaring Brook Press
- St. Martin's Press
- Griffin
- Minotaur
- Thomas Dunne Books
- Tor
- Forge
- Orb
- Starscape

It is entirely possible that, with this new development, other major publishers that are in competition with Macmillan might adapt this same strategic move, which would serve to further open up the opportunity for independent authors to discover a whole new world of readers through the library.

The BIG DEAL about Large Print

Many authors who have their book available in the three formats of print, eBook, and audiobook believe that they have covered all the formats.

But there is another print format that can be a massive thing for libraries.

Large Print books.

Yes, the advent of eBooks means that every single reflowable eBook is, essentially, a large print book (readers can modify the font style and size directly in their eReader or the app that reads the ePub or mobi file). But since a huge amount of the population still has not read an eBook, libraries are still on the lookout for large print editions of books.

Creating a large print book is a bit different than the process of creating a standard print book. But you do have options that don't require a lot of research and background study. The Apple based eBook creation tool *Vellum*, for example, has some built-in large print creation options. And *IngramSpark* does offer large print format options within POD.

There are, of course, costs involved in creating large print versions of your books. But it's also an activity that can set you apart from the competition.

Imagine that a library is looking to fulfill a specific style or type of book for a demographic that only wants these books in paper and in large print format. Your book's availability in that format could be the deciding factor on a sale, or loss of a sale.

Leaving Your MARC

A detail that I purposely skipped over in this chapter (mostly because I felt that the details and overview might be too complicated already), was explaining MARC references and their importance to libraries. And, even so, what I'm sharing here is extremely high level and gets nowhere near close to the full details.

A **MARC** record is a **MA**chine-**R**eadable **C**ataloging record.

A Cataloging record refers to the *Bibliographic* records (containing information about a book), and *Authority* records (containing standardized forms for names, titles, and subjects, providing cross-reference in catalogs). Additional formats include *Classification* records, *Community Information* records, and *Holdings* records, which often have more to do with internal classification and specific product holdings that are location (library) specific.

MARC was developed in the 1960s in the United States as a way for computers to be able to read records about books and other library materials for cataloging. By the early 1970s MARC formats became the library industry standard in the US; and by the mid 1970s, they evolved into an international standard.

While libraries can and do make purchases on titles that lack MARC records, some libraries may be reluctant to create MARC records. This might be from a combination of the labor and setup costs involved.

If your book is traditionally published, chances are that your publisher either has direct account or is using a service to have MARC records created. If you are self-published, a MARC record might not exist. Some countries have subscriptions, memberships and services that allow entry of MARC records. Depending on where you live and the resources available, you might have limited ability to ensure a MARC record exists for each format of your book. But I didn't want to talk about libraries without at least briefly mentioning this.

If you are looking for more information, I have provided a few links in the resource section at the end of this book. I have also provided a bit more information at www.markleslie.ca/authorsbookstoreslibraries.

The Value of Public Lending Right

This particular section is only going to pertain if you live in a country like Canada or the UK, or Australia, or one of the more than thirty countries around the world that have public lending right programs.

And, if you do, then it is very important for you to understand how it works and why it can be extremely valuable for you as an author.

What Is Public Lending Right?

Public Lending Right is the right of authors and other rightsholders to receive payment for the free public use of their work in libraries.

PLR has been in existence since the 1940s. The very first library compensation program of its type was established in 1946 in Denmark. Norway was second to establish one in 1947, as did Sweden in 1954.

As of 2019, thirty-five countries have PLR programs. Of these, thirty are in Europe. Outside of Europe, only Australia, Canada, Israel, and New Zealand have PLR systems.

Internationally, PLR is overseen by an organization known as Public Lending Right International (or PLR International). The aim of PLR International is to promote international awareness of PLR and inform the PLR community of events, developments and news from around the world. It brings together those countries with established PLR systems and provides assistance and advice to countries interested in setting up PLR schemes.

You can learn more about PLR international at plrinternational.com.

How Does Public Lending Right Work?

In most countries, PLR is directly funded by government budgets that are controlled either centrally or regionally. The currently existing thirty-five programs fall into three broad categories:

- Copyright-based systems where lending is the exclusive right
- PLR as a separate state renumeration right recognized by law
- PLR as part of state support for culture

Some countries incorporate a combination of all three of those approaches.

How Are Payments to Authors Calculated?

The most common method of PLR is distribution to authors or other stakeholders in the form of payments related to how often their work has been lent out by libraries. Alternatively, payments are calculated to rightsholders via a tally of the total number of copies of their books held by libraries. This particular method is used in countries such as Australia, Canada, and Denmark. Countries like France base their calculations on sales from booksellers to libraries, with part of the funding coming from the bookstore and the remaining part of the budget coming from the government according to how many users are registered in the libraries.

Who Qualifies for Payment of PLR?

Writers qualify for payment of PLR. So do other contributors to books, such as artists and illustrators, editors, photographers. In some countries, publishers receive a share of the PLR payments.

Details from Canada's PLR Program

Because I am a Canadian, and because I am most familiar with, and have benefited from the way the program works in Canada, I will outline how the program works in my country.

I know that the programs in the UK and Australia, for example are different, such as in Australia, at the time of this writing, the PLR program is only for print books, or that in the UK, there's a 60/40 split on audiobooks for author/narrator. But these things continue to change and evolve.

For the most up to date understanding of how PLR works in your own country (including Canada), should you be an author lucky enough to have a program like it, you can learn about it via your country's direct PLR program website, which you can find at the following URL:

http://plrinternational.com/established

Canada's PLR program was established in 1986. In Canada, PLR payments are based on the presence of a title in public library catalogues, as tallied during an annual PLR survey. The calculation is determined by the PLR Commission, which is an advisory board of the Canada Council for the Arts. The process of paying authors takes a full year and involves four main steps:

- Registration of titles
- Verification of title eligibility
- Sampling of public library collections
- Preparation and distribution of payments

The registration period for Canadian creators is between February 15 and May 1st each year. You must be a Canadian citizen or a permanent resident to be eligible. Writers, illustrators, translators, narrators, editors, and photographers are eligible.

Books in print, eBooks and audiobooks that have been published in the previous five years are eligible. The print book or eBook must have a valid 13-digit ISBN and must be at least 48 pages long (or 24 pages in the case of a children's book). Audiobooks must be in either a physical media format (CD), or a digital download (MP3) and have a valid 13-digit ISBN.

Fiction, poetry, drama, children's literature, non-fiction, and scholarly work are all eligible.

Practical books, such as cookbooks, self-help, "how-to" guides, travel guides, manuals, and reference works, are not eligible. Educational books, such as textbooks or books resulting from a conference, seminar, or symposium, are not eligible. Periodicals, such as newspapers or magazines, are not eligible.

There can be no more than six contributors to the book, and the each creator's contribution must comprise of at least 10% of the length of the book.

Sampling of eligible titles is done by including libraries with large collections from all provinces, territories, and regions of Canada. Neither the number of copies found on hand, nor the number of times a title has been checked out are considered; merely the presence of that title in each particular location that is sampled.

At the end of the process of comparing eligible titles to the online or digital copy of library catalogs, a tally of the number of times each eligible title appears is calculated.

Payments for each title are based on the library sampling results, the creator's percentage share of the title, how long the title has been registered with the program, and the amount of money in the program's budget and the total number of eligible titles.

The calculation formula is:

Payment per title = Hit rate × # libraries where title is found × % share × time adjustment

The "hit rate" changes every year. For 2018 the "hit rate" was $58.90. The sampled libraries will be a number between 0 and 7. The time adjustment involves the number of years a title has been registered. If registration was in the past five years, for example, it is 100%. For six to ten years, that drops to 80%.

Only those creators whose library survey results amount to at least $50 qualify to receive a payment. The maximum possible payment varies each year. In 2018 it was $4,123.

A Personal Example of Canada's PLR

I have been registered with the PLR program in Canada for at least ten years. I actually can't remember when I first registered. And, because the registration program isn't tracked online via a database, but rather via a printed form that you have to mail, I don't have an accurate record of what books were registered in what year.

All I have are copies of the annual statements that have been mailed to me along with an annual check.

Just this past year, I began making a photocopy of each newly submitted form, as well as logging, in a spreadsheet, when the print, eBook, or audiobook was published and submitted; this is to ensure I know which books were submitted, and when.

I remember that the very first payment I received from PLR was relatively small. But, over the years, as I have continued to publish more books, and in more formats (PLR Canada only added eBooks to the program recently), those annual checks have grown significantly.

In 2019, for example, my Public Lending Right check, which arrived in late February, was large enough that it paid for my all-inclusive flight, meal and drink plan for a tropical vacation.

I remember it quite well because, the credit card statement for that particular March Break trip and the check from PLR Canada arrived around the same time.

If you happen to live in one of those territories that has a Public Lending Rights program, I strongly encourage you to sign up for it.

TIPS, IDEAS, AND STRATEGIES FOR SUCCESSFUL IN-PERSON BOOK EVENTS

THIS CHAPTER PERTAINS mostly to the brick and mortar retail locations of libraries and bookstores, but it could also apply in virtually any in person event that you do in other venues.

Whether it is a book signing, a talk, a workshop, or a vendor table at a local craft fair or convention, the way that you behave, interact with others, and present yourself prior to, during, and after the event, can make a huge and lasting difference.

For that reason, I wanted to make sure that I listed a number of ideas, suggestions, and examples of things that I believe can help you in being seen as a professional by the booksellers, librarians, event organizers, and readers that you interact with for these events.

Put on Your Author Face

I know that most writers are introverted by nature. We prefer to spend our time in front of a keyboard making stories up. But in person events require coming out of that shell.

It's not easy. You might be sitting at a table at the front of a bookstore and watching people walk by, simultaneously terrified by the worry that nobody is going to stop to talk to you and look at your books, or that people *are* going to approach you. Because, if they do approach, what do you say? What if they reject you?

It's never easy. No matter how many times I've done in person events, I have to overcome my desire to slip back into that introverted default position, or to put away any of the negative things that I might have been carrying with me.

From the minute you get into the store, try to remember that you are representing your overall author brand. You want to be seen as a professional.

A smile is a little thing, but it can make a huge difference. While perhaps not as contagious as a yawn, it is a subtle visual element that can infect others with positivity.

If it helps, remind yourself of the hard work and effort you put to write the book and get it published. Remind yourself that everybody thinks they have a book in them, but very few write one. And for the ones who write them, very few have published them. And for the ones who have published them, very few are doing an in person event as an author.

That's a pretty amazing accomplishment.

Worth smiling about, no?

In the early days of my bookselling experience, I had an excellent manager who reminded us that when we were at work, and on the sales floor in front of customers, we were expected to be a bookseller. Not a student worried about a forthcoming exam, not a jilted boyfriend or girlfriend; not someone who stayed out too late and partied too hard the night before. None of that negative baggage. There was a back room, off the sales floor, where we could be angry, curse, and even hit a blow-up punching bag that he had put in there. But when we stepped onto the sales floor, we were to put on the persona of the world's best bookseller.

It reminded me of my days of acting when I was in university.

And it worked extremely well.

I carried that with me for the rest of my bookselling career. And I also carry something similar with me when I'm making an appearance either as an author or as a book industry professional.

So, when you're out there, think about the fact you are an author, a published author, who has overcome so much just to be where you are. And wear that with pride. Channel that "best author in the world" spirit and own it.

Something that I found extremely helpful and which you might benefit from is Todd Herman's book *The Alter*

Ego Effect: The Power of Secret Identities to Transform Your Life. I walked away from reading this book with some amazing ideas and strategies for helping me get my game face on in the appropriate situation, regardless of what inner turmoil or fears might be working to hold me back.

Could you have a persona that exemplifies an outgoing, confident, champion author, one who is perfectly fine with speaking to strangers, entertaining a crowd? Does having that persona become the person who is exposing themselves or making themselves vulnerable to rejection – rather than it being personal, rather than it being about you – an easier way to allow yourself to slip into that role?

A Winning Attitude

It might feel that I'm harping on about a similar point to the one that I made above, but I'm only doing so because it's important.

I guarantee that, no matter how many events you do, no matter how many books you might have sold overall, there are going to be events that are a complete bust. Where not a single book gets sold, or not a single customer shows up.

I have had it happen to me multiple times.

And each time I've had it happen, I can fret over the fact that I wasted an entire day, or spent a significant amount of money to travel to a distant location, only for the whole thing to be a bust. Or, I could be grateful for the opportunity to meet new people, to have time to get to know and chat with the booksellers or librarians.

In one particular event, where I had been doing a tour of a new release, I arrived at a Vancouver bookstore. The bookstore, my publisher, and I had all broadly shared and advertised the event in local print media, in flyers, in store posters, and social media. And yet not a single customer showed up for my book signing and talk. In fact, it was a quieter than usual night for the store, and barely any customers showed up. The bookstore staff were extremely apologetic about it and I assured them that, having worked for years as a bookseller, I knew that these things could happen, and it was out of everyone's control.

I took advantage of the two hours I was at the store to get to know the booksellers, to assure them that I was not angry or upset, and that I understood that these things happen. And, when they asked, I shared a few stories related to the writing of the book, as well as some of the content that I had planned on sharing in my talk. We also discussed a few of my other books, completely unrelated to the one that was recently released, as a part of that conversation.

We had a good time; I got to chat with them about their favorite reads, and some of my own favorite books. It was not all that different than the fun book talk I had engaged in with my bookstore colleagues on quiet times when all the tasks were done and there were no customers around.

I didn't sell a single book that night, but I'm willing to bet that, at some time not too long after that day, those booksellers remembered me, the book I was featuring, and are likely to have, for the right customer, talked about me or my books with them.

A sentiment that has been attributed to Maya Angelou, H. Jackson Brown and Carl W. Buehner says that people might forget what exactly you said, people might forget what exactly you did, but people will never forget how you made them feel.

Does your behavior make the people you are interacting with feel positive or negative?

Pre-Promotion

If you are going to be either a featured author or appearing with others in any sort of event, make sure that you have taken the time to share it in the ways that you can. Letting people in your community know, adding it on your blog or website, mailing the info via your author newsletter, posting about it on social media, and, where appropriate, tagging the bookstore, library, or venue where you will be appearing, so they know that you are promoting the event and promoting them, too.

In the case of a multi-author event, tag the other authors, their new books – share generously and graciously.

For some events, you can consider doing a Facebook live, Instagram story or even a short YouTube video talking about the event, about the venue, about the other people that might be there with you. Sharing the event shows the bookstore or library that you are actually engaged in promoting the event and their location.

Get the Lay of the Land

First, if it's a location you have never been to before, either make sure to get to it prior to the event itself (in the case of a local spot that you have ongoing or easy access to), or arrive a bit earlier than you are expected, so that you have some time to scope things out.

In one way, particularly if you are nervous about putting yourself out there, if the introvert in you or the internal voice that reminds you how much you hate public speaking or selling or whatever it is, sometimes knowing the space you'll be operating in, as well as the space around it, might bring a sense of comfort, or control to your mind.

But it's also a way for you to become familiar with the locale.

When I'm at an inside location such as a library or bookstore, I try to determine a few key things. Where the restrooms are; where the main sections are (new releases, bestsellers, fiction, the children's books, etc); what other shops are nearby. When I'm at a craft festival or comic-con style event, one in which there are plenty of other vendor tables, I try to become familiar with a bunch of other nearby authors or even other products, complimentary or not.

Why would I go to the effort?

For those chance encounters that have nothing to do with you and your books.

And it will happen.

All the time.

Some of the people who approach you, sitting at an author table inside of or at the front entrance to a mall bookstore, don't see an author sitting at a table with their book or books – they see a person who might be an employee and can be helpful.

They might ask you where the restrooms are.

They might ask you about a new and popular book. Or where a particular section of the bookstore is.

You have two main choices when such things happen. You can be offended, or you can be helpful.

Being helpful likely also helps the staff of the store; but it also improves that customer's experience too.

I also like to, where I can, get to meet as many of the staff members as possible, even just briefly. It's likely often just a single person who has been your contact prior to the event, or is perhaps your contact during the event. But there are likely other staff members around. Those working the sales floor, those working the cash desk.

If you arrive early, you might have the chance to chat with them a little, get to exchange some information.

Why can that be important?

On one basic level, they can learn just a little more about you or about your book. You can help inform them of the content beyond the title, the back cover copy, etc, so they are better equipped to talk about you and your book when a customer who is leery of approaching your author table can get the info they're curious about without approaching.

On another level, it could help you. Let's say you learn that one staff member, Ellen, for example, is a huge fan of young reader urban fantasy, and that another staff member, Bob, is a giant sports fanatic, and a huge fan of the local baseball team. You suddenly have multiple touch points to bring value to the browsers and shoppers who stop to talk to you; particularly if your book and its topic is nowhere in their ballpark.

I'll use me and my books as an example.

A lot of the book signings that I do are related to the non-fiction paranormal true ghost story realm. Explorations of local history and ghosts associated with a local. Those books are not everyone's cup of tea.

Some people want to talk to me, not because they are interested in my books, but they are fascinated with talking to an author. It never hurts to be pleasant and helpful to them. And, in our conversation, if I learn that they came to the store looking for a great read for their niece or nephew who loved the Harry Potter books, I might be able to let them know they should seek out Ellen, because I'm sure she'd be able to recommend something great. Or maybe the man I'm talking to is wearing a Blue Jays ball cap or I observed him browsing a book on the history of baseball before he came to talk to me. I could ensure that he chats with Bob, who can likely tell him more about the book.

Because half the time, or more than half the time, the customer, the browser, the shopper, doesn't realize there is a book event, or book signing taking place. And they will assume that you are an employee of the store.

It's not their fault. It's part of the normal day to day expected experiences in their life. In the average retail shopper's experience, how many people responsible for the creation of the product are standing there able and willing to talk about the product they played a hand at bringing to market. (Well, apart from those folks offering free samples of a new convenient lunch snack item or demonstrating the magical wonder of that never-dull set of knives on sale today).

For many people, they don't expect you to be the author. They expect that you work there; and thus know things. And thus can be helpful.

Here's another scenario.

I'm sitting at the front of the bookstore in a mall. Nobody has stopped to talk to me. I'm still nervous, and tense, wondering if the entire time spent setting this up and sitting there is a complete waste of time.

Suddenly, from across the mall, a middle-aged gentleman looks over, sees me at the table. His eyes widen, as if in recognition or intrigue. He immediately heads my way with a purposeful stride.

I begin to feel a sense of quiet pride. Something about me and my book table have impressed him. Finally, a customer who is interested.

He arrives at the table, and in a hurried voice, asks where the nearest restroom is.

I'm deflated. I mistakenly thought he was interested in me. But, like many customers, all he saw was someone he thought was an employee of the store. His eyes lit up not because he was interested, but because he saw me as a solution to his current problem, his current need.

I can let that be the end and say I don't know, I'm just an author.

Or, I can smile and graciously provide the answer to the very genuine question he asked.

I've done this hundreds of times.

And here's the interesting thing. Half the time, once their urgent need or issue is addressed, they open up and then see what's going on, the situation, and understand I'm not an employee. Other times, perhaps well after they have attended to their urgent need (in the case of a restroom visit), they are relaxed and take in the viewpoint and understand.

I've had people either immediately catch on, or some time after, return to say thanks; or return to apologize.

"Don't be sorry." I say in response. "Glad I could help."

Expecting that to be the end of our transaction has, many times, resulted in a now non-rushed person who engages in genuine conversation, and, sometimes, interest. We might discover that me and my books are right up his alley. Or we might recognize that they are not in his wheelhouse of interests. But he knows something that he plans on telling about me and my books – and it'll likely be a positive sharing.

There are also plenty of times that people coming up to my table at a comic con are definitely not interested in my ghost story books, or my thrillers, or horror fiction titles. But I can see, based on their cosplay costume, or some other purchased product they are holding, that they are fans of epic fantasy. I can helpfully inform them of a fellow author who has a great series of books about dragons that I think they might like.

Being friendly; being helpful; ensuring the customers who come into the store feel welcome; playing an active role in a way that enhances the experience of store customers in some small way. These are all far more valuable than you might at first suspect.

It leaves an overall positive impression of your visit to that store for both the customers and the staff, even at an underlying and sub-conscious level.

And in the worst-case scenario, you did something to make someone else's day better.

So, you'll always have that.

Nobody Likes to Be Sold To

One of the odd paradoxes of being successful at selling is not actually selling. It's about making the right connections.

At least that's how I have always seen it.

I don't like selling; I never have.

But I like connecting with people.

So that is what I focus on.

I rarely do or say anything to make the person I am speaking to feel pressured to buy. That backs them into a corner and more likely leaves them with a negative impression of the experience. Even if they end up buying a book, they may resent the manipulation that led to it rather than be thrilled with the idea of reading my book when they get home.

You might notice that people will be interested by the sight of you sitting at a table with a pile of your books in front of you. You can often tell, from the look on their face, that they are intrigued and curious, and are filled with a desire to come over. But sometimes they don't. And that's likely because, along with that compulsion is a niggling fear that they are going to be sold to.

This is why I do whatever I can to alleviate that fear.

If I'm trying to draw someone in that I think is interested, I don't usually toss out a line about buying my books, but I might pitch out a line related to an intriguing story that might draw them in.

It could be something generic. But I find that an intriguing gem that gets them to think can work nicely.

For *Haunted Hamilton*, I might say something like: "Would you like to hear why I call this book my love letter to the city of Hamilton?"

For my thriller *Evasion* I might say: "Imagine that everyone you knew or met was trying to kill you. Where would you hide? How would you escape?"

If there is a fundamental or universal question to your book, that might be a good way to get a conversation going. A genuine back and forth exchange. It might lead to a sale. It might not. It's quite likely that the person speaking with you isn't interested in reading or in your books. But what is likely, if you make some small connection, that they'll remember you. And, if they know someone who might be interested in your book, they might share that with them at a future date.

Or it might just be that perhaps you helped ensure there was a moment in their day that they connected with someone.

I can live with that. At least I was part of a pleasant exchange in their day and not some smarmy salesperson they had to confront.

So a lot of what I do when I'm at my author table, is talk with and engage with people.

And, while closing the deal is apparently a good sales tactic, I typically prefer one that is more about offering them something rather than trying to sell them something.

Thus, I often prefer to say something like: "Can I sign a personalized copy for you?" rather than "Would you like to buy a copy."

Better No Sale Than the Wrong Sale

A book in the right hand is worth two on their bookshelves at home.

That was my vague attempt at trying to re-draft the old "a bird in hand" saying.

Or, another way of saying this is that I would rather not get a sale if that sale wasn't to the right person who would be very likely to read and enjoy that book.

Because I'm not interested in just moving units, in making a sale today. Because if I do force that sale today, I get a single unit moved and a single sale, but that's where it ends.

However, if I sell the right book to the right person, that single sale could lead to multiple repeat business of my other books in the future.

Instead of a single sale, I might have gained a single reader, or a single fan.

This is directly related to engaging and connecting with people, which I spoke about above. As part of the exchange that I have with people, I often ask them what they like to read.

If their answer is a type of book that is completely outside of the realm of my offerings, I never try to pull them in and get them interested in my books. But I will, if I know something that I think they might genuinely enjoy, tell them about other books. Perhaps it's a book from a friend, perhaps it's something I've read that I think they will appreciate.

There is no point in me trying to sell one of my thrillers, urban fantasy, or ghost story books to someone who is looking for a solid police procedural novel. So, if I learn that is what the customer is interested in, I politely let them know my books are likely not their cup of tea but might share how much I enjoy Michael Connelly's Harry Bosch novels.

Or, if the customer in front of me loves romance, and enjoys specifically reading second chance romance, I'll tell them about my friend Julie Strauss's awesome Oro Beach novella *Almost Blue*.

In fact, I have sometimes talked people out of buying one of my books if I felt that it wasn't the right fit. For example, my horror novel *I, Death* is chock-full of intense violence and extremely adult content. I've had people wanting to buy a copy for their fifteen-year-old who likes creepy things and I've talked them out of it, warning them of the intensity of the content, that I believe should be flagged as for those eighteen or older. If I can, I'll suggest something that is dark and eerie, but doesn't have that kind of graphic sex and violence in it. But the last thing I want is for them to get the wrong book.

Sell Only to Your Target Audience

I know that I stated this in slightly different words, but I think it's a critical notion and one that bears repeating. Particularly because we can be so proud of our books and our writing, that we forget not everyone is our target audience or intended reader.

The last thing I'll ever believe is that my books are great for everyone. Horror is not everyone's cup of tea, so I'm used to the plain and simple fact that my target demographic audience is smaller than those interested in romance or thrillers or mysteries – yes, there might be some cross-over, but I am aware that my stuff doesn't appeal to everyone; nor should it. Any author who believes their book is great for everyone is demonstrating that they haven't really thought their target audience out yet.

I am aware that a book such as *Haunted Hamilton* can appeal to three types of people:

1) Those who love ghost stories and tales of true supernatural events.

2) Those who love history, particularly local history.

3) Those who love anything having to do with the city of Hamilton.

Fortunately for this book, that's a pretty broad target demographic. However, I do recognize that there are those who simply won't be interested in it. But they most certainly might know someone who is.

It is critical for an author to recognize that fact -- and yet, so difficult for some to realize, particularly since us authors tend to be pretty passionate about our work, our babies.

When I'm at my table sure I'm enthusiastic about and eager to discuss my book -- but I also pay attention to the person in front of me. And if it's not clear to me that they'd be interested, I come out and ask what kind of things they like to read. If historic ghost stories of the local area aren't of interest to them, then I'm honest and might tell them a little but suggest they wouldn't like it. This gives them an easy "out" if they're not interested and doesn't waste my time nor their time.

I think one of the worst things is if someone who isn't interested in the topic or genre ends up buying it. It'll most likely *not* be a pleasant experience for them, and they're more than likely going to tell everyone they know that you and your book suck. They'll go on to leave a one-star review of the book. None of that is what you want.

But if someone who is likely to enjoy what you've written purchases your book, chances of them liking it are dramatically improved. Which can lead to additional future sales, positive reviews, and that person enthusiastically telling their friends about it.

You have enough hard work to do as an author. Why stack the odds against you by starting off with the wrong sale?

Prop Yourself Up

It all started, for me, with Yorick, a ceramic tea light skull I had bought at a craft fair.

My first book, *One Hand Screaming*, featured a close-up of my eye on the cover with the eerie image of a skull reflected in it. The book contained eerie *Twilight Zone* style stories. So, the skull was a fitting prop.

I ended up continuing to populate my author table when doing events with other macabre items, including a black tablecloth with either spider-webs or skulls, and even a tombstone or two propped up in front of my table. That eventually led to the acquisition of Barnaby Bones, my life-sized skeletal companion who now accompanies me on most of my author events.

These props serve a few purposes.

Obviously, they call unique attention to my author table; particularly when I'm doing an event outside the Halloween season.

But they also pretty clearly let anyone walking by know the genre or content of my books. So this allows them to either take a wide berth as they walk past ("don't make eye contact with the creepy horror author"), or be immediately drawn to talk to me and check out my books.

Another thing this does is it offers people a fantastic icebreaker. Barnaby is often sitting right beside me at my author table.

At every event, plenty of people come up to me to comment on how my friend looks like he could use a meal, or maybe that he has been sitting there a long time.

Yes, it's a joke I've heard hundreds of time.

But it's likely the first time this person has thought of it and made that joke.

And it is funny.

So, I smile, I laugh, and I usually quip something back.

It breaks the ice. We joke, we chat. Sometimes it leads to a discussion about my books. Sometimes it leads to a sale. But it very likely also led to that person telling someone about their experience with the tall bald dude and his skeleton friend.

Often, people ask if they can take our picture, or take a selfie with Barnaby. Sometimes Barnaby even has a t-shirt on with the cover of the latest book I have released. The sharing on their social media of that selfie with Barnaby brings with it extra eyeballs becoming aware of my book. Free advertising. I'll take it.

Another recent acquisition that I try to hang in a visible spot is a bat-shaped "Ghost stories told here" sign. It's another visual cue that informs potential readers what some of my books are about. And another eye-breaker.

I'll often have someone point at the sign and say, "tell me a ghost story." Because I've written hundreds of them, I usually respond with asking what sort of ghost story they prefer. A historic one, one from a local building, a humorous one, etc. And then I share.

It's another great conversation starter.

You might be thinking that my example is an outlying one that works well for my genre or is an easier thing to pull off because of the ease of sourcing Halloween style decorations. But what it comes down to is finding a theme or element from your book or books that can be visually unique and appealing.

When my friend, author Suzy Vadori released her YA novel *The Fountain* she appeared at numerous bookstore and library events with a three-foot-high 3 tier water fountain. She offered people a chance to toss a prop coin into the fountain and to make their wish, just like Ava Marshall, the heroine of her novel. Suzy's use of this unique prop is not only eye-catching, but it involves interaction and engagement.

A Little Thanks Goes A Long Way

After the event is over, make sure to thank the staff, offer to help them tidy up, put chairs and other event items away, or other mundane tasks.

Bookstores typically don't make much money at the average event. Sure, they might sell some books, but many times there are costs you as an author don't see. They have to order extra stock, receive and unpack the stock - set up a display/table, potentially advertise or produce posters or flyers for the event. Then, when the event is over, they have to send the overstock back to the publisher, which also costs time, resources and money. If you're a consignment author the work is even more manual and often frustrating for the staff/management, typically because it's a different system that requires extra effort outside the normal daily processes.

In a nutshell, having an event is a lot of work. I know this because I've been a bookseller for several decades. I know the work involved.

Thus, if, after the event, you take the time to write a simple thank-you card and send it to the manager/owner, it goes a long way. Perhaps there was a staff member there who did something special, made you feel great, was personable, friendly, great with customers. Take the time to make sure you compliment them, praise them in some way; ideally in writing. It'll make the manager/owner feel good about their store and about their staff.

And it never hurts to have a bookseller, bookstore manager/owner like you. When deciding which title to put in the front window, on a limited space display, and the choice ends up being between your book and some other book that fits equally well, how do you think your previous positive kind actions will affect that decision? How about when it's time to get rid of extra stock to clear shelf space. Will it be your book or another title? How will your interactions with them affect that?

One year, I took Barnaby Bones to a visit to Santa. I made up Christmas cards of him sitting on Santa's knee, and I sent those cards to every library and bookstore I had interacted with in the previous year. It was just a simple wish for them to have a wonderful holiday season, and perhaps something humorous that they would remember me for. "Oh yeah, that guy with the skeleton."

One of the most wonderful examples of gracious and giving thanks happened when I was at a comic con in Sudbury, Ontario. Fellow *Cambridge Authors* writer Richard H. Stephens and his wife Caroline were there at the table beside mine with his epic fantasy novels.

Throughout the day, whenever they interacted with the staff and volunteers at the con, they were pleasant, and gracious, and thankful.

When, at the end of the day, they were packing up their books, signage and other swag, they took the time to leave behind a note of thanks for the volunteers who would be coming along to collect the tables and chairs and booth hardware.

They'd been to a number of cons and knew how hard so many different people work. I imagine that whoever got to that table, someone who was likely tried from working an extremely long day (much longer than the long day us author vendors had), seeing a simple note acknowledging and thanking them likely made a huge difference to them.

Newsletter Sign Ups

When I first started doing book signings, it was a good idea to have a clipboard with a pen so that people could jot down their name and email address to be added to my monthly author newsletter. Sign-up to the newsletter often comes with the reader receiving some sort of special subscriber only offer or deal, like a free story or free eBook.

If you are unfamiliar with author newsletters, this is one of the best ways to ensure that you are in contact with your readers and fans, rather than relying on your publisher or a retailer for that. One of the best books on author newsletters I've ever read is *Newsletter Ninja* by Tammi Labrecque.

A clipboard was, back in the day, a handy tool. And it can still be. Because it's simple and easy. But sometimes the writing can be hard to interpret properly; it can also be extra work (inputting that info); and with the anti-spam double-opt in systems of newsletters, it can be a bit tricky.

So you might consider just doing something like sending an email within 24 hours of your event to the people who gave their email. Thank them for visiting you at the table – if this was a customer you had a fun exchange with or who you know bought one of your books, thank them for that conversation or the purchase. And, in that email, remind them about the newsletter and let them know they can sign up – often for a special offer or deal made available only to subscribers to your free newsletter.

If WiFi is available, a tablet connected to the internet that links directly to your newsletter sign up page can also work nicely.

Additional Options & Gives

Pretty much all of my books are available in eBook format. Some are available in audio.

If I am speaking with a customer in front of a pile of my print books and they mention that they only read eBooks, I let them know my books are available at all retailers, in eBook format.

If I am in a specific store that has a website that carries the eBooks (Chapters/Indigo in Canada, for example, carries Kobo eBooks; hundreds of indie bookstores in the US have eBooks powered through either Kobo or Hummingbird) I suggest they check out the bookstore's website to find the book(s).

This can come in handy because the eBook is usually a better price than the print book. So a customer who is price conscious knows they have that option.

I sometimes also bring printed over-sized postcards with the book cover of one of my books on the front and the book description blurb on the back. And I include a link to where they can download the eBook for free. It is often through a great service like Bookfunnel.com.

Depending on where you are, this can be tricky. This free giveaway is something I'm careful about when I'm in someone else's retail space. A free giveaway at my author table at a comic con or craft fair is one thing. But it might not be as acceptable in a retail bookstore.

It might be something you only do with permission from the hosts. And do always try to remember it from their perspective. For example, if you are in an independent bookstore, be leery about overtly sending customers to a competitor. Standing in an independent bookstore and directly customers to Amazon is rude, insulting, and a major slap in the face to the bookstore that has invested time and energy into your appearance there.

With the release of my book *Tomes of Terror: Haunted Bookstores and Libraries* I was appearing at three different bookstores over a weekend. Two of them were independent bookstores. One was a chain. The other appearances were at a library.

I created some t-shirts that had an image from the book cover on the front, along with my website URL. On the back of the shirt was the message: "I like to haunt" followed by the name and logo of the bookstore or library I was appearing at and their website URL. Below it, the shirt had the question: "What's your favorite bookish haunt?"

I printed off ten of each custom location shirt in different sizes. Barnaby wore one (appropriate to each location), and I gave a few others to the owner or store manager so they could give them to the appropriate regulars or loyal customers. I also held onto a few to give to any really enthusiastic fans.

The t-shirts advertised the bookstore, but also my book. While measuring the effectiveness of such a move is difficult, I did interact with a few fans who, like me, were giant book nerds, loved the idea of a book about haunted book locations, and were beside themselves with joy to own and proudly wear such a shirt; especially one that advertised their favorite local bookish haunt.

The Proximity Paradox

Remember how I talked about how people might look over and be intrigued or interested in your books. Heck, if, like me, you have highly visible props to get the attention of the right people, that might increase the potential interest.

But, often, particularly in bookstores, you are dealing with introverts. They are happy to come in and look for a great book to read. But they're less comfortable engaging in conversation and definitely do not want to be sold to or have to deal with some sort of fearfully anticipated "sales pitch."

So, something that I like to do when doing a bookstore signing, is ask the staff if it's okay for me to have a small display at least ten feet away from my table. Or perhaps it's a small display near the cash register with a sign that says: "In store today. Meet Mark Leslie, author of *Spooky Sudbury*."

This type of display that is not in front of a live author allows those people who want to check it out, but are a little bit leery to approach, wander over to check out the books with absolutely no pressure.

At one bookstore event I did, there was a display of my books less than ten feet away – again, far enough away that people could check out the book without feeling me hovering over them. This allowed them to relax and casually enjoy the experience of browsing or learning what my book was about, without the sense that

I was expectantly waiting to talk to them, interrupt or throw a hard sales pitch at them.

I noticed that several different people who were initially "afraid" to approach me and took a wide berth of my table, paused to check out my books on display further away.

About 75% of the time, upon browsing the book without stress, they would approach me at my table and ask if I was the author and if I could sign the book. Without that display, they likely would have just moved past, curious but not inching close enough to realize it might be something of potential interest to them.

Confidence, Not Cockiness

One last thing to remember when you are engaging staff, volunteers, and readers, is that you have already accomplished something pretty significant.

Most people will say that they want to write a book. One day. Most won't. And of the people who do actually write a book, a good many of them will not have had that book published – through either traditional or self-publishing.

And of the ones that are published, an even smaller number will be out doing an in person book event.

So that does make you unique, and someone who has overcome multiple hurdles.

Even if it's an event with few people and few or no sales, it's still an amazing achievement. And it's okay to wear that with pride.

Be careful not to fall prey, though, to the monster of "comparisonitis." Looking at those who have done better, or been in the game longer. At times, looking there and thinking about working on the path to get there can be inspiring.

But it can also be a frightening walk down the path to lack of confidence.

My friend Robert J. Sawyer offered me this advice many years ago and it's something I have taken to heart. He said that it's important to define yourself as a big fish in a small pool.

I write horror. So if I compare myself to Stephen King, one of the biggest fish in the horror community, I'm going to feel insignificant.

So, in the global realm, I'm perhaps not a big deal.

But as a horror writer in Waterloo, or Hamilton, or Ottawa, or Sudbury (four cities I've called home), I stand out a bit more, might be seen to have a bit more relative success.

Heck, I'm the only horror author that I'm aware of from Levack, Ontario, a town north of Sudbury of approximately 2000 people where I grew up. So I could likely say that I'm the top bestselling horror author from Levack, Ontario.

Do your best to show up with confidence and pride. You are the best person to have written and shared the book that is in front of you. You worked hard to get there.

You overcame so many obstacles along the way. You are unique. Your book is too.

Just try not to get so confident, so cocky, that you lose all humility, all manner of being kind and thoughtful, and generous. Be confident, but be considerate to other authors, to the booksellers and librarians who are your partners, and to the readers, who you engage with, on the page, online, and in person.

CONCLUSION

THIS BOOK IS, in many ways about making connections with others in the industry. Booksellers, librarians; and, ultimately, readers.

This book is also the result of a connection that I have made with a group of important people. The listeners to my podcast *Stark Reflections on Writing & Publishing*. At the time of this writing, I'm well past 100 episodes of the weekly podcast that has been running since the beginning of January 2018. The focus of the podcast is on different elements of the business of writing and publishing that I have learned over my decades in the industry, and that I am continuing to learn. I share my learnings, my experiences, and my reflections on what I'm doing and learning, with my listening community.

My listeners will often send me messages or leave comments asking me to cover different topics or discuss specific things. One of them was an episode about interacting with bookstores. Another was a similar episode talking about libraries.

My listeners appreciated and enjoyed that content. But I kept thinking about it, and realized that there was likely more I could do in that realm.

So I took the transcripts of those two episodes and laid them out onto the digital page. Then I started digging into further details, fleshing out some ideas. That inspired other concepts, other things I thought would be important to share.

And that lead to this book.

So, this book wouldn't have happened without that connection, without that wonderful community. Among the many amazing listeners from that weekly extended family I connect with, I'd like to thank Rachel Amplett, Caro Begin, and Chad Boyer for their comments, suggestions, asking great questions, and helping to inspire the content and topics for this book.

My hope, now that you have come to the end of the book, is that you have found something of value; something informative, something insightful, something inspirational. And that you are able to take that, to considerate it within the context of your own unique writing life, writing and publishing goals, and adapt it into something that you can use on your unique writer journey.

RESOURCES

BELOW YOU WILL find a short list of some of the resources called out in this book, as well as ones I have found helpful in my own writing and publishing journey.

I also maintain an online listing of these resources, as well as examples and templates, at:

www.markleslie.ca/authorsbookstoreslibraries

Books

5 Critical Things for Successful Book Signings, Adam Dreece, ADZO Publishing Inc., 2019.

Business for Authors, Joanna Penn, Curl Up Press, 2017.

Million Dollar Professionalism for the Writer, Kevin J. Anderson & Rebecca Moesta, WordFire Press, 2014.

Dealbreakers: *Contract Terms Writers Should Avoid,* Kristine Kathryn Rusch, WMG Publishing, 2013.

Mastering Amazon Ads, Brian D. Meeks, Brian Meeks, 2017.

Killing It on Kobo, Mark Leslie Lefebvre, Stark Publishing Solutions, 2018.

Newsletter Ninja, Tammi Labrecque, Larks & Katydids, 2018.

Strangers to Superfans, David Gaughran, David Gaughran, 2018

The Successful Author Mindset, Joanna Penn, Curl Up Press, 2016.

The Seven P's of Publishing Success, Mark Leslie Lefebvre, Stark Publishing Solutions, 2018.

This Business of Publishing, Richard Curtis, Open Road Media, 2014.

Podcasts

BookNet Canada Podcast
www.booknetcanada.ca/podcast

The Career Author
www.thecareerauthor.com

Kobo Writing Life Podcast
www.kobowritinglife.com/category/kwl-podcast

Sell More Books Show
www.sellmorebooksshow.com

Six Figure Authors
www.6figureauthors.com

Stark Reflections on Writing & Publishing
www.starkreflections.ca

The Creative Penn
www.thecreativepenn.com

The Self Publishing Show (formerly The Self Publishing Formula)
www.selfpublishingformula.com/spf-podcast

Writing Excuses
www.writingexcuses.com

Website Resources

The Alliance of Independent Authors
www.allianceindependentauthors.org
www.selfpublishingadvice.org/self-publishing-service-reviews

Audiobook Production Platforms
Authors Republic Listing
www.authorsrepublic.com/creation
IPG Audiobook Production Contacts
www.ipgbook.com/audiobook-production-contacts-pages-925.php

Canadian ISBN Service System (CISS)
www.collectionscanada.gc.ca/ciss-ssci/app

Independent Bookstores
Biblio.com
www.biblio.com/bookstores
AU
Australian Booksellers Association
www.booksellers.org.au
Australian Independent Booksellers
www.indies.com.au
CA
New Pages
www.newpages.com/independent-bookstores/canada-bookstores
Retail Council of Canada
www.retailcouncil.org/resources/tools/find-a-bookstore-map
UK
Booksellers Association – Bookshop
www.booksellers.org.uk/bookshopsearch
US

American Booksellers Association & Indiebound
www.bookweb.org
www.indiebound.org
NZ
www.booksellers.co.nz

Kobo Hacks for Optimizing Sales (Free Email Course)
www.blog.reedsy.com/learning/courses/distribution/kobo-hacks

Kobo – Maximizing Your Sales at Kobo (Article)
www.selfpublishingadvice.org/maximizing-your-sales-at-kobo-by-mark-lefebvre-director-of-kobo-writing-life-author-relations

Kobo – How To Sell More Books on Kobo (Video)
www.youtube.com/watch?v=xSZVlEJi5E8

LibWeb (Library Servers via WWW)
www.lib-web.org

Library Review Magazines
Booklist
www.ala.org/aboutala/offices/booklist/insidebooklist/booklistproc/proceduressubmitting
Library Journal
www.libraryjournal.com
Publishers Weekly
https://www.publishersweekly.com
(Publishers Weekly - BookLife)

www.booklife.com/
School Library Journal
https://www.slj.com
Voya
http://voyamagazine.com/publishers

Universal Book Links
Books2Read
www.books2read.com
Book Genius
www.geni.us
SmartURL
www.manage.smarturl.it

Public Lending Right – PLR International
www.plrinternational.com/
www.plrinternational.com/established

Writer Beware
www.writerbeware.com

ABOUT THE AUTHOR

Mark's highly successful experience in the publishing and bookselling industry spans more than three decades where he has worked in almost every type of brick and mortar, online and digital bookstore.

The former Director of self-publishing and author relations for Rakuten Kobo, and the founding leader of *Kobo Writing Life*, Kobo's free direct-to-Kobo publishing tool, Mark thrives on innovation, particularly as it relates to digital publishing.

He writes full time and mentors and coaches authors and publishers about digital publishing opportunities both 1:1 and via his Stark Reflections on Writing & Publishing weekly podcast.

You can learn more about Mark at *www.markleslie.ca*

Selected Books by the Author

Under the name Mark Leslie Lefebvre

Writing & Publishing

The 7 P's of Publishing Success

Killing It on Kobo

An Author's Guide to Working with Libraries and Bookstores

Under the name Mark Leslie

Non-Fiction ("Ghost Stories")

Macabre Montreal

Haunted Hospitals

Creepy Capital

Tomes of Terror

Spooky Sudbury

Haunted Hamilton

Fiction

Nocturnal Screams (Short Fiction Series)

A Canadian Werewolf in New York
Evasion
I, Death
Active Reader: And Other Cautionary Tales from the Book World
One Hand Screaming
Bumps in the Night

As Editor
Fiction River: Superstitious
Fiction River: Feel the Love
Fiction River: Feel the Fear
Fiction River: Editor's Choice
Tesseracts Sixteen: Parnassus Unbound
Campus Chills